PLAY
THE GAME

PLAY
THE GAME

Compiled by Brian Love

Michael Joseph
and
Ebury Press

ACKNOWLEDGEMENTS

The author and publishers wish to thank the following individuals and organizations for their help in the preparation of this book:
Bodleian Library, Oxford (John Johnson Collection)
Graham Bush (photographer)
Chad Valley Company Limited, Birmingham (The Chad Valley games reproduced in this book are from the author's collection)
Mrs Barbara Harvey Loynes, daughter of F.R.B. Whitehouse
National Trust (Waddesdon Manor, Aylesbury, Buckinghamshire)
Museum of London
Norfolk Museum Services (Strangers Hall, Norfolk)
Victoria and Albert Museum (Bethnal Green Toy Collection)

First published in Great Britain by
Michael Joseph Limited
44 Bedford Square, London WC1
and
Ebury Press
National Magazine House
72 Broadwick Street
London W1V 2BP
OCTOBER 1978
SECOND IMPRESSION DECEMBER 1978
THIRD IMPRESSION SEPTEMBER 1983

ISBN 0 7181 1724 7

Printed and bound in Belgium by
H. Proost & Cie, Turnhout
Made by
Roxby Press Productions Limited
98 Clapham Common Northside
London SW4 9SG
Editor
Michael Leitch
Design
Pentagram
Production
Reynolds Clark Associates Limited

CONTENTS

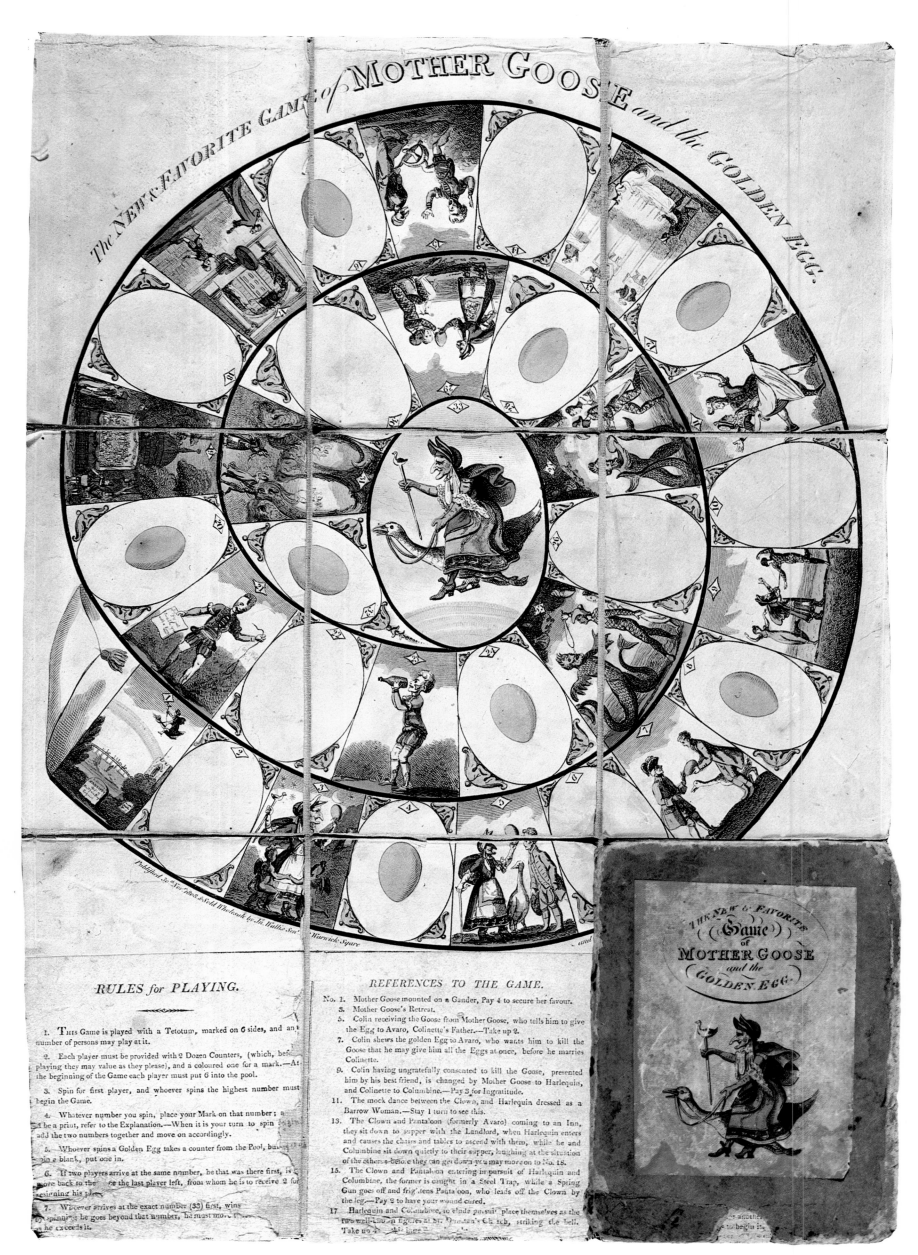

The NEW & FAVORITE GAME of MOTHER GOOSE and the GOLDEN EGG.

RULES for PLAYING.

1. This Game is played with a Tetotum, marked on 6 sides, and any number of persons may play at it.

2. Each player must be provided with 2 Dozen Counters, (which, before playing they may value as they please), and a coloured one for a mark.—At the beginning of the Game each player must put 6 into the pool.

3. Spin for first player, and whoever spins the highest number must begin the Game.

4. Whatever number you spin, place your Mark on that number; a ... be a print, refer to the Explanation.—When it is your turn to spin ... add the two numbers together and move on accordingly.

5. Whoever spins a Golden Egg takes a counter from the Pool, bu ... spin a blank, put one in.

6. If two players arrive at the same number, he that was there first, is ... move back to the ... the last player left, from whom he is to receive 2 for ... resigning his pl ...

7. Whoever arrives at the exact number (33) first, wins ... spinning he goes beyond that number, he must move ... as he exceeds it.

REFERENCES TO THE GAME.

No. 1. Mother Goose mounted on a Gander, Pay 4 to secure her favour.

3. Mother Goose's Retreat.

5. Colin receiving the Goose from Mother Goose, who tells him to give the Egg to Avaro, Colinette's Father.—Take up 2.

7. Colin shews the golden Egg to Avaro, who wants him to kill the Goose that he may give him all the Eggs at once, before he marries Colinette.

9. Colin having ungratefully consented to kill the Goose, presented him by his best friend, is changed by Mother Goose to Harlequin, and Colinette to Columbine.—Pay 3 for Ingratitude.

11. The mock dance between the Clown and Harlequin dressed as a Barrow Woman.—Stay 1 turn to see this.

13. The Clown and Pantaloon (formerly Avaro) coming to an Inn, they sit down to supper with the Landlord, when Harlequin enters and causes the chairs and tables to ascend with them, while he and Columbine sit down quietly to their supper, laughing at the situation of the others before they can get down you may move on to No. 18.

15. The Clown and Pantaloon entering in pursuit of Harlequin and Columbine, the former is caught in a Steel Trap, while a Spring Gun goes off and frightens Pantaloon, who leads off the Clown by the leg.—Pay 2 to have your wound cured.

17. Harlequin and Columbine, to elude pursuit place themselves as the two well-known figures at St. Dunstan's Church, striking the bell. Take up ...

THE
PRINTED GAME

The 46 gameboards that readers can play in this book have one thing in common: they all first appeared in printed form. The earliest in our collection date from the latter part of the 18th century. They were printed on paper, like maps, from engraved copper or steel plates, and were coloured by hand with water-colour paint.

It is rare for copies of the same 18th-century game not to show variations in the colour schemes employed. Each was an individual product, and publishers usually allowed their colourists reasonable freedom to vary their treatments as the fancy took them. Colours could be made constant by using stencils, but for the most part they were applied freehand with a brush. Shortly before 1840 lithographs began to replace the engravings of the early publishers, though some of these also were coloured by hand.

The earliest dated game known in Britain: 'A Journey through Europe or the Play of Geography', invented and sold by John Jefferys in 1759. The countries are hand-tinted with pale washes of water-colour, and the game was originally contained in a slipcase. The game is played in the same way as games of 'Goose' (see examples below).

For presentation and sale to the public, these early gameboards were mounted on canvas or linen after printing (as a safeguard against tearing), and were then folded and enclosed in a slipcase. The slipcases were made of stout paper or thin cardboard covered with a marbled or fancy paper; a printed label was then affixed to the outside. Folding covers later took the place of slipcases. These were usually made of cardboard covered with cloth, the latter blocked with the title of the game and various ornamental details.

The rules of the game were featured on or beside the gameboard, and sometimes appeared in expanded form in a separately printed book of rules. These were small in format but could be fairly extensive. If a game featured forfeits or instructional passages on most of the numbered spaces, this would be reflected in the length of the rulebook. In 'Wallis's New Game of Universal History and Chronology' (1814), for example, an event from history is described on every one of its 138 panels, and the book of rules, listing the forfeits and conveying supplementary information about some of the more notable events, runs to 34 pages.

The completed games were put on sale in the shops of their inventors and publishers. Many of the London games publishers made their living principally as map and print sellers, and operated from addresses in the purlieus of Fleet Street, Ludgate Hill and St Paul's Church Yard. No records can be found of the quantities printed of particular games, but it is reasonable to assume that editions of successful, i.e. popular, games amounted through reprints over a period of years to several hundreds or even thousands of copies.

Label affixed to the folding cover of 'The Travellers of Europe', published in 1852 by William Spooner.

In his book Table Games of Georgian and Victorian Days (London, 1951), F.R.B. Whitehouse notes that a booklet issued with 'A Companion to Betts's Portable Globe' contains a list of the firm's games and the declaration that 'The demand for these games has now reached the Twelfth Thousand.'

Such a sizeable quantity indicates a considerable public appetite for games. Armed with a small library of amusing and instructional boardgames, the parents and children of pre-electric times could enliven the long winter days, spinning the tee-to-tum and racing each other round a numbered serpent or spiral until

Decorative label on sliding box-lid for a 19th-century geographical game, 'Ships & Commerce or Merchants of the Mediterranean' (Standring & Company, 1860).

one of them arrived, with ritual cries of delight, at the Conqueror's Castle or whatever device marked the winning post, and with still greater glee collected the contents of the pool.

Wallis's slipcase and gameboard for 'New & Favorite Game of Mother Goose and the Golden Egg' (1808).

ANCIENT AND CLASSIC BOARDGAMES

The printed games of the 18th and 19th centuries are a formalized and more widely diffused version of something very much older. Men have played competitive boardgames for more than 4,000 years. The earliest known gameboard employing the familiar cells or panels of the conventional race game was found in a cemetery near Abydus in Upper Egypt; conical playing pieces were also found on the site, which dates back to 4–5000 BC. In tombs of the 9th and 12th Dynasties (spanning the years 2445–1801 BC), boards have come to light that were made for a game known as 'Dogs and Jackals'. This was a race game not unlike 'Snakes and Ladders', one of the favourite boardgames of modern times (first registered in 1892).

Nearly all boardgames share a number of common features. Most are played by 2 or more people or by 2 opposing teams of 2 or more players. In some games the pieces are arranged in a fixed pattern on the board before play begins; in others, the players may choose their own arrangements, and place their pieces on the board either alternately or simultaneously; in yet others, the players enter a few pieces at the beginning of the game and keep the rest in hand for use later. In the majority of games, once the order of play has been determined and the opening round of moves concluded, the players then move in turn until a winner emerges. He or she is usually the first to achieve a given aim, e.g. the first to reach some sort of winning post, or the first to conquer or eliminate a given number of opposing pieces.

The surface of play is generally a board marked out according to the conventions of a particular game. The various chequerboard patterns used for 'Chess', 'Draughts', 'Halma', and many other games are some of the most familiar designs. Other common types feature either panels or

Classic label and gameboard, with rules in a centre panel, for 'The Game of the Race and Steeple-Chase'.

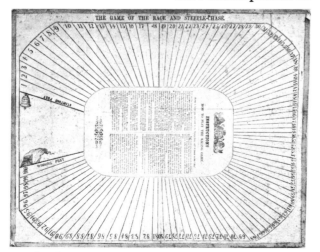

marked-off spaces, often numbered and arranged in some spiral, serpentine, rectangular or random pattern. The chequerboard pattern is usually employed for

strategic 'war' games; of these 'Chess', in one or other of some thirty variations, is the best-known example. The various other forms of gameboard, the spirals, snakes, etc., commonly denote race games employing a single track which all players follow.

In ancient times, and among technologically less advanced societies, the playing surface might be made of any of a number of convenient local materials, or be marked out on the ground. One such game, known as 'Hyena', evolved among the Baggara Arabs of the Sudan. They made their boards by tracing a spiral pattern in sand, which was then pierced at random intervals by holes.

Illustration of Chad Valley's 'Globe Ludo' game from the company's first games catalogue for 1897-98. This popular game originated in India as 'Parcheesi' and was brought to the West in the late 19th century.

Each hole represents a day's journey; a larger hole at the centre of the spiral denotes a well, and at the beginning of the track, on the outer edge of the spiral, a 'village' marks the starting point. Each player takes a marker that represents his mother. For scoring, dice are used that consist of 3 short pieces of stick, split so that one side shows white, and the other a darker colour. The 3 sticks are tossed in the air and score as follows: 1 white side up – a taba; 2 white sides up – score 2 and the turn ends; 3 white sides up – score 3. Each player must throw a taba before his mother can leave the village on her way to the well. The players throw in rotation and may continue throwing until a 2 is scored.

The game plan of 'Hyena' is typical of many of the route-and-race games appearing in the later pages of this book (from page 18 onwards). Another ancient race game is 'Parcheesi', its title derived from the Hindi word pachis, meaning '25'. Virtually a national game in India, it is played there in cafés and public places as well as in private homes. It was developed originally from the Korean game of 'Nyout', and reached the West in the late 19th century as the still-popular game of 'Ludo'.

GAMES OF 'GOOSE'

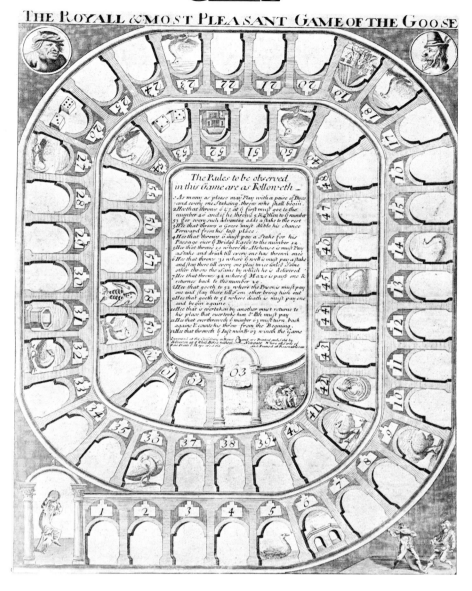

One of the archetypal race games, which has inspired scores of offspring, is the game of 'Goose'. It is likely that the ancient Greeks had a boardgame on similar lines, but the man usually credited with popularizing the modern version is Francisco dei Medici (1541–87). The Giuoco dell'Oca ('Game of Goose') became widely known in Europe in the late years of the 16th century, and was taken up with particular avidity in France.

The French were keen games players, and they developed it as the Jeu de l'Oie in various ways. On a piece of cardboard, the Jardin de l'Oie ('Goose Garden') was drawn up, usually in a spiral or snail-shell pattern, along which the players advanced their counters from space to space until the winner arrived in the centre; on numbered tracks the Home space was usually No. 63. In typical examples, the way was snared with various hazards which required fines to be paid and rewards received, in token form, either to or from a central pool or the other players. It was a convention, too, that anyone landing on a space featuring a picture of a goose was obliged, in the words of an English version, to 'duble his Chance forward', i.e. to move forward again by the same score until he came to a goose-free space. Another popularly observed rule was that the winner was entitled to take the contents of the pool.

Games of 'Goose' were well received at Court. King Louis XIII of France played it as a child; the Grande Dauphine turned it into a gambling game at Versailles, and in England the Duchess of Norfolk was sufficiently enthused to plant out a garden version, using hornbeam, in her park at Worksop.

The basic game pattern was borrowed for many other kinds of geographical, moral and religious game. In 1759, for example, the cartographer John Jefferys referred to it in his 'Journey through Europe or the Play of Geography', in which he instructs the players to 'proceed as in the game of Goose'.

One of the most exuberant examples is Wallis's 'New & Favorite Game of Mother Goose and the Golden Egg' (1808). The players race round a short spiral course from Nos. 1–33: anyone arriving on a Golden Egg may take 1 token from the pool; along the way a crowd of popular comedy figures – Harlequin and Columbine, Clown and Pantaloon – await the players, with varying awards and penalties.

Towards the end of the 19th century, the Baron de Rothschild gathered together a unique collection of French boardgames dating from between 1675 and 1820. These are now kept at Waddesdon Manor, near Aylesbury, Buckinghamshire. The majority of these games are variations on the 'Goose' concept, some having pronounced satirical or political overtones; several are illustrated in these introductory pages.

Early example of an English game of 'Goose': 'The Royall & Most Pleasant Game of the Goose', published by H. Overton c. 1750.

Maps and mapmakers have always exercised a strong influence over the development of boardgames. Indeed, most of the early publishers of games founded their businesses on cartographic productions and prints. By the beginning of the 19th century those publishers had found that there were profits to be made from educational games. Geography was an obvious field for them to exploit, and instructional games that set out to teach children about the shapes of countries and continents form a large and significant group.

Rather more subtle than those, though not to everyone's taste, were the earlier allegorical maps and map-influenced designs that flourished in France from the late 17th century onwards, when preciosity enjoyed a long run of popularity among courtiers and their middle-class imitators – and writers such as Molière and La Rochefoucauld drew savage pleasure from debunking them.

A French allegorical map, the Carte de l'Isle du Mariage (1732).

The idea of the 17th-century novelist, Mademoiselle de Scudéry, for a Carte du Tendre in which emotions became place names in a saccharine world of the romantic imagination, had many imitators. In the Waddesdon collection referred to above, for example, is the Carte de l'Isle du Mariage (1732). The largest island in its imaginary archipelago, set in the Ocean of Melancholy, is the Island of Marriage. It is divided into regions entitled the Land of Cuckoldry (in which the chief residence stands), the Country of Ennui, and various other sectors, the majority representing states of unhappiness. Smaller seas, those of Hope, Visions, and Disgust,

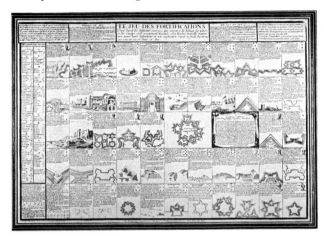

A French military game, the Jeu des Fortifications (1712), designed to glorify the military installations of Sébastien de Vauban.

are included, and the main island is surrounded by a chain of smaller islands, all named after emotions or states of being. To the left lies the mainland, where the Kingdoms of Pleasure and Freedom are separated by the River of Wills. Although it forms part of the Waddesdon collection of Jeux, it is unclear whether the Carte de l'Isle du Mariage had formal rules or was intended only as an exercise for the imagination, to be mooned over by leisured matrons.

Other Waddesdon games are more explicit about their uses. One of these is Les Etrennes de la Jeunesse ('The Gifts of Youth'). This is a romantic game played on a 'Goose' pattern, but with 2 circles or tracks: the men, or cavaliers, race from 1–32 around the left-hand track, while the ladies follow the other track. The hazards are designed to involve both sides; thus, if the man arrives on Indiscretion (No. 28), he must allow his lady bergère ('shepherdess') to bind a handkerchief over his mouth and knot it behind his head until he is pardoned; he must also pay 1 token.

The French were also adept at converting games to political ends. The func-

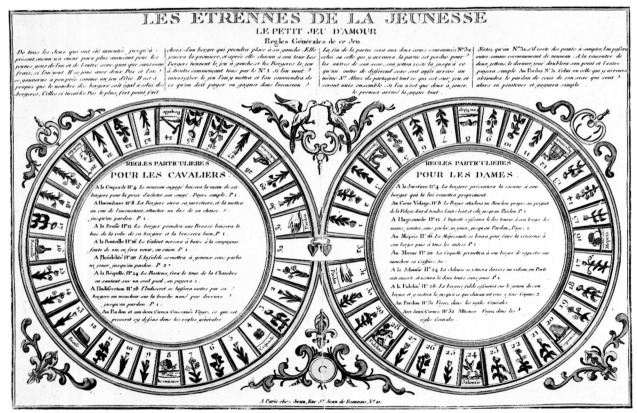

Les Etrennes de la Jeunesse ('The Gifts of Youth'), a romantic French game modelled on 'Goose' but with 2 circles or tracks, 1 for players of either sex.

tion of the Jeu des Fortifications (1712) was not only to amuse but also to display the designs of the great military engineer, Sébastien de Vauban. As a game, one of its interesting aspects is that it may be played either with dice, when it becomes a variant of 'Goose', or with the different sections cut out to form a pack of cards.

Slipcase and gameboard of the 'Walker's Tour through England and Wales' (1809).

Another military game, the Nouveau Jeu de la Marine (1768) is superficially a game of 'Goose' with a maritime slant, but its central purpose was to promote the renascent French Navy in the eyes of the young, and to capture recruits. In the main Games

section of this book, on pages 40–41, is a further example of a French propaganda game, the Jeu de la Révolution Française (1791); again, the pattern is that of a game of 'Goose'.

The value of games as methods of instructing the young was fully appreciated by a French priest who took refuge in Britain from the excesses of the Revolution. He was the Abbé Gaultier (1746–1818), and in his country of exile he found rewarding support for his ideas. Many of these materialized in an important publication (and forerunner of Play the Game) entitled 'The Abbé Gaultier's Complete Course of Geography, by Means of Instructive Games'.

The 'Course' took the form of a 50-page book illustrated with 14 maps, 7 of which were in outline only while on the other 7 the various place names were fully marked. A set of counters was provided, bearing the corresponding names of kingdoms, provinces, islands, seas, rivers, etc., which the pupil-players deployed to prove how well or otherwise they had absorbed the information given in the fully documented maps.

In time, similar teaching aids were produced to help children to better their

grasp of English, French, History, Classical Mythology, Natural History, Arithmetic and Astronomy. Morals and Religious

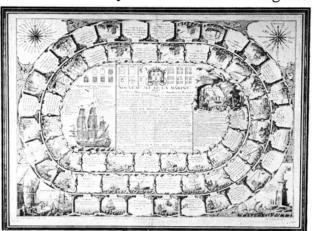

The Nouveau Jeu de la Marine (1768), a 'Goose'-type propaganda game whose object was to draw recruits to the French Navy.

Knowledge were other fields that the publishers eagerly explored. As the market for games (and also toys, but that is another story) expanded, so the publishers sought to capitalize on the mood of the times by devising games that were little more than out-and-out moral tracts for the young.

A prime example is 'The New Game of Virtue Rewarded and Vice Punished' (see also pages 30–31). Published in 1818 by William Darton of London, it requires each player to run the gauntlet from Nos. 1–33, from the House of Correction to Virtue. Since arrival on any space earned doses of either praise or castigation, no player could hope to finish unmarked.

Another moral game, published in London by John Harris in 1815, is called 'The Swan of Elegance'; this game consists of 31

Folding cover and gameboard of an American Bible game ('for Sundays') called 'Bible Pastime', designed by Mary C. Whitney of Tokyo and Anna Braithwaite of Baltimore, Maryland.

circular spaces, each containing a picture of a visibly 'good' or 'bad' child. It is played with a teetotum (or spinner) and counters, and in the accompanying booklet of rules there is a verse for each space. This is how visitors to 'Idle Jane' are received:

Now, pray, is not Jane a true emblem of sloth?
See! how idle she lolls in her chair;
She still must remain in the seat where she is
Till the Totum's spun twice by each play'r.

FORTUNE'S FAVOURS

Chance has a major hand in most board-games. Of those appearing in the Games section of this book, the only exceptions are the strategic games, such as 'Halma' or 'The Siege of Paris', in which the players make simple alternate moves by a number of spaces, usually 1 only, as defined by the rules. For non-strategic games, an impartial arbiter is needed to determine the extent of each move. Most commonly, a die or 2 or more dice are thrown, rolled, flipped or tossed from the hand or a cup to provide players with the answers they seek. In this act parallels can be seen with an earlier function of dice. Before they became gambling implements, dice were magical objects and were employed in sortilege, the casting of lots to divine the future.

The other principal form of arbiter used in boardgames is the tee-to-tum (or teetotum, or totum, or spinner). This is a development of a children's top, has 4 or more sides, and was common in games of moral improvement introduced in the 18th

and 19th centuries, when public opinion in some quarters was inclined to equate dice with gambling, and by extension with evil, ungodliness, etc.

Whatever their ethical merits, the teetotums produced results equivalent to dice. In William Spooner's game 'The Journey' (1830s), the totum is referred to as the 'Circle of Chance'. In the 18th century totums were made from turned bone or ivory; in later times, a piece of card was used, which the players pierced at the centre, inserting a matchstick or similar object on which the totum could pivot.

To return to the subject of dice, those that concern us are the cubic or 6-sided variety. Dice did have other shapes: in the British Museum, for example, are Roman dice with 14 and 20 faces; in the main, however, it was customary to use a teetotum when a selection of numbers greater than 6 was required. The standard die thus has 6 faces, each of which is marked with 1 to 6 small dots or spots. The

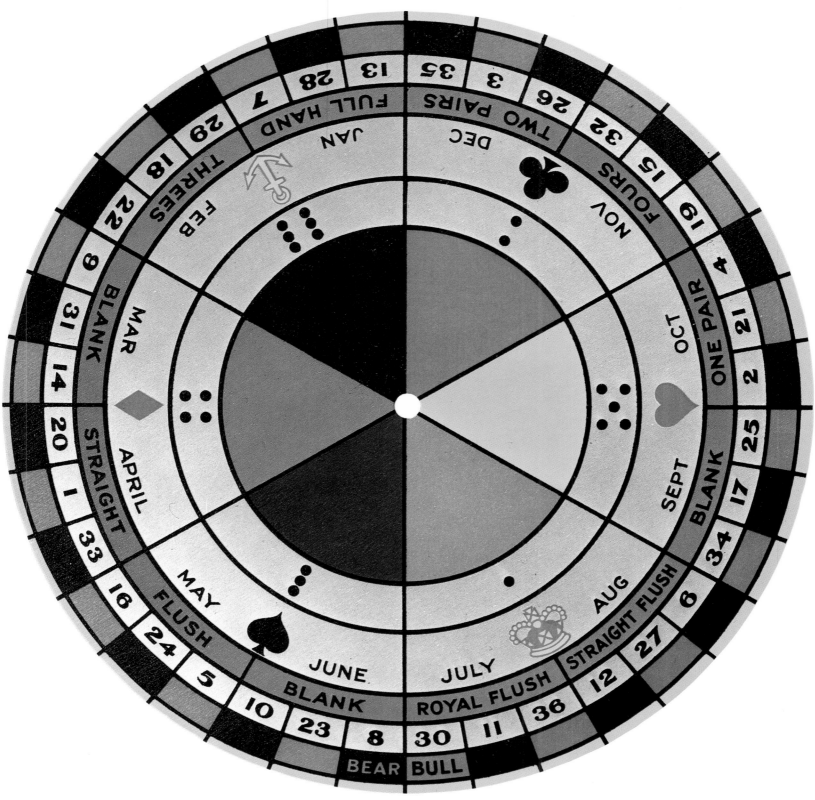

spots are arranged in conventional patterns, being placed so that the spots on opposite sides always total 7, i.e. 1 and 6, 2 and 5, 3 and 4. Modern dice are mostly made of plastic and consist of 2 kinds: 'perfect' or 'casino' dice, used in gambling casinos, and round-cornered or 'imperfect' dice, known also as 'drug-' or 'candystore' dice. The latter kind are used for social boardgames such as appear in this book.

The probable forerunners of dice were knucklebones (ankle bones of sheep) marked on 4 faces. In Arabic the word for a knucklebone is the same as that for a die. Ethnic groups from all parts of the world – from the first inhabitants of the Americas to South Sea islanders and Africans – for centuries have gambled with dice made from numerous kinds of materials. They used seeds, plum and peach stones, moose and buffalo bone, deer antlers, pebbles, earthenware, walnut and cowrie shells, and many others.

In Greek and Roman times most dice were made from bone and ivory, while others were of bronze, agate, rock crystal, onyx, marble, amber, porcelain and other substances. Cubic dice with markings equivalent to those of modern examples have been found in ancient Egyptian tombs made some 4,000 years ago. There is also evidence that some early Egyptians threw 'staves' rather than dice or knucklebones. Examples were found in Tutankhamen's tomb which, in type at least, may be related to the sticks of the Sudanese Arabs discussed earlier.

The other instruments of play used in boardgames are the counters or markers by which each player traces his position on the gameboard, and the tokens used for paying 'stakes', etc. In Europe, coins were once used as markers, but the risk of loss soon brought about the introduction of brass counters. These were manufactured in considerable quantities at Tournai in France, in the Netherlands, and in Nuremberg, Germany; many of these were designed to resemble coins. The British were slow to enter this trade, but during the reign of George III (1760–1820) several English button and token manufacturers applied themselves to producing counters for the gambling and boardgame markets.

A marvel of the gramophone age: both sides of Mead & Field's 'Casino Crackers' (c. 1928), a spinning compendium offering 8 games in a folder. Players put the spinner on a gramophone turntable, span, and then made their moves on the accompanying board according to the disc's position when it stopped.

The appeal of boardgames grew at a steady pace throughout the 19th century. Their range also expanded with the introduction of novel gameboard patterns such as the 'cross-roads' type (see pages 52–55) and another reflecting jig-saw puzzles. Towards the end of the century 'shopping' games were to prove another popular genre. Not unlike present-day 'Housey-Housey' or 'Bingo' games in concept, they require the players to collect pictorial tokens associated with particular trades or commodities. These are laid down on blank circles on the gameboard, and the winner is the first to make up a complete set. One such game was brought out by the firm of Chad Valley, and features various trades, among them the Fruiterers, the Grocery Stores, the Jeweller, the Milliner and Draper, and the Toys and Games shop.

Chad Valley also helped to enlarge the field of 'abstract' games. These employ a gameboard on which there is no obvious or representational target, but usually a variety of possible routes is offered, along which the players race each other from point to point, or attack each other's pieces as in strategic games of the 'Chess' family. 'Quinto', published by Chad Valley in 1905, is an example of an abstract gameboard; here the influence of 'Ludo', not long introduced to Europe, is apparent.

The increased volume of business demanded industrialists rather than small cartographic businesses to handle the trade. The gentle salesmanship of the shopowner-pub-lisher was replaced by the more pressing tones of the sales representatives who radiated from their respective factories, where thunderous machines such as Dr N.A. Otto's gas engine powered the mass creation of gameboards, tokens, boxes and all that went inside them.

In 1811, John Harris issued a Christmas catalogue that is steeped in the old world's ways of small-scale trading. It states: 'Christmas Presents and New Years Gifts, Harris (late Newbery's) the corner of St Pauls Church Yard, begs leave to announce to the Nobility, Gentry and the Public in general, that he has recently printed the following little books for the Instruction and Amusement of Youth; and that he has always on sale a general assortment of the publications written by Mrs Trimmer, Mrs Lovechild, the Abbé Gaultier and other esteemed authors; of which a Catalogue consisting of many hundred articles, will be delivered gratis.'

At about the same time as John Harris was seeking to interest people in his books and games, Anthony Bunn Johnson was setting up a printing and bookbinding business in Birmingham. By 1860 his sons were running a firm called Messrs Johnson Bros which specialized in the production of stationers' sundries, including labels and envelopes. In 1897 Joseph Johnson, one of the brothers, was running the business assisted by his eldest son Alfred. They moved the company to a new factory in the village of Harborne, just outside Birmingham.

Charming example of a 'shopping' game, published by Chad Valley. The players collected tokens and placed them on the appropriate circles, racing each other to complete a shop card.

Building on a theme: how Chad Valley attacked the burgeoning sport of motoring with their range of race and chase games.

At Chad Valley's Harborne works in 1905:

The Engineering and Toolmaking Shop.

The Box-making and Games Department.

The Printers' Composing Room.

The Bookkeeping and Accounts Department.

The Labelling and Dispatch Section.

Johnson Bros delivery van (previous livery of firm).

There, beside a stream known as the Chad, they set up the Chad Valley Works and introduced into their range of goods a selection of cardboard games. From then until the 1920s, when the soft-toy trade outgrew all the other segments of their business, Chad Valley produced scores of charmingly designed boardgames. It was a golden age of graphic design, and these early products, many of them featured in the Games section of this book, are now rare collectors' items.

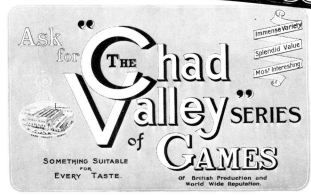

Chad Valley carton label showing the company's factory at Harborne, Birmingham, c. 1900.

For a time after 1914, when all imports of toys and games ceased, Chad Valley and the other English gamemakers enjoyed a captive market. The German naval blockade also meant that supplies of strawboard from Holland were no longer available. The inventiveness and artistry of the games' designers, and the skill of the

venturous in the post-war era. Special promotions were organized in hotels and restaurants such as the London Ritz, and actors and other well-known personalities were enlisted to demonstrate the wares in these pastures of the wealthy. This was how in 1923 Chad Valley launched their version of 'Mah-Jongg', sometimes known as the

Chad Valley catalogue illustration promoting 'Am-Duat', an Egyptian version of 'Mah-Jongg', which the company launched in 1923 together with its own version of Chinese 'Mah-Jongg'.

CATALOGUE OF AM-DUAT (THE EGYPTIAN MAH-JONGG) AND 1924 PATTERNS OF MAH-JONGG.

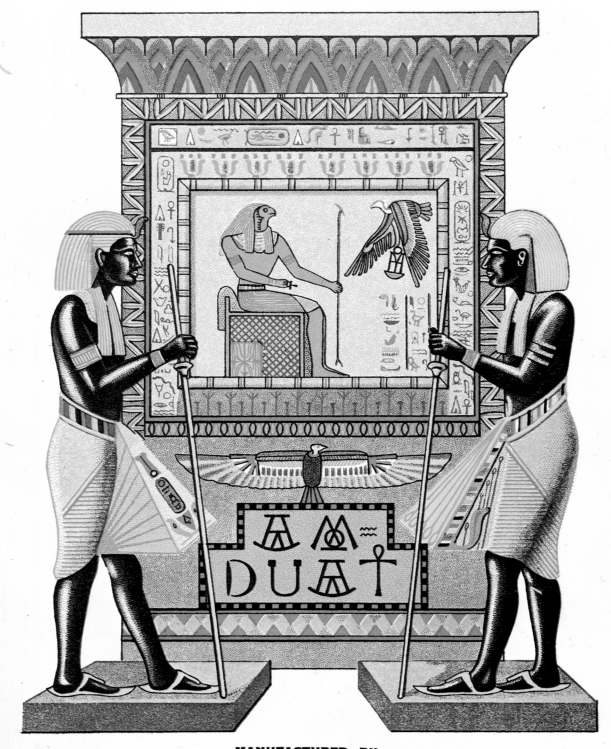

MANUFACTURED BY

THE CHAD VALLEY Co., LTD.,
HARBORNE,
ENGLAND.

printers and boxmakers, were evidently unaffected, however, and in 1919 the factory was in need of more space. Chad Valley Works extended into the Harborne Village Institute, which was taken over and laid out as a printing works to provide the box covers and labels for the games and other products.

Marketing methods were more ad-

Chinese game of 'Dominoes', which they brought to Britain from America. They were charming, never-to-be-repeated times; but today we can still take enormous pleasure from the colour and style of the gameboards, admiring their agreeable symmetry as we endlessly recreate the excitement of playing the games. And so, aptly, to page 17.

On the following pages
are 46 games, each with its
own gameboard, set of
numbered rules, and a brief
historical introduction.
To play the games,
first cut out and collect the
necessary counters,

THE

GAMES

tokens, etc., from the pocket
at the back of the book,
using the Checklist of
Moveable Pieces on page 96
to make sure you have
everything you will need. Then
open the book at the game
page, lay it flat on a table
. . . and play on.

LAURIE'S NEW AND ENTERTAINING GAME OF THE GOLDEN GOOSE

This Victorian game was published in London on 22 November 1848 by Richard Holmes Laurie of 53 Fleet Street. It is based on a much older game that originated in Italy. Called the Giuoco dell'Oca ('Game of Goose'), it was probably invented at the time of Francisco dei Medici (1541–87). He sent a version to Philip II of Spain, through whose patronage the game spread to other parts of Europe. It had certainly reached England by 1597, for on 16 June that year John Wolfe entered 'the newe and most pleasant game of Goose' in the Stationers' Register.

The game is played along a serpentine course of 63 points, which are consecutively numbered. Any number of persons can play, and the moves forward are determined by throwing 2 dice.

The rules listed below do not differ substantially from those in the oval of the gameboard. Some minor amendments have been made, as elsewhere in the book, in order to present the various rules in a reasonably consistent style.

1   This is a game for any number of players. Each is provided with a counter of a different colour, and an agreed number of tokens to pay 'stakes', etc. All players should begin with the same number of tokens.

2   The order of play is determined by throwing the dice. The highest scorer begins, the second highest goes next, and so on.

3   The players throw the dice in turn and advance by the total indicated. The game path begins at the Golden Goose's head (No. 1) and finishes above its left leg (No. 63).

4   Various hazards are as follows. If a player arrives on No. 6 (Bridge), he must pay 1 token and go to 12. If he arrives on a Goose, he must double his score, i.e. move forward by the amount shown on the dice; if this brings him onto another Goose, he must double his score again, until he is free of Geese. If he arrives on No. 19 (Alehouse), he must pay 1 token and drink there till his turn comes to throw again. If he arrives on No. 31 (Well), he must miss 2 turns unless someone else arrives on No. 31, in which case the new arrival takes his place and he goes to the other player's old space. If he arrives on No. 42 (Maze), he must pay 1 token and go back to No. 29. If he arrives on No. 52 (Prison), he must pay 1 token and stay there until his place is taken by another player arriving on that number. If he arrives on No. 58 (Death), he must pay 1 token and return to the Start.

5   If a player is overtaken by another, both must pay 1 token and the former must go to the other player's old space.

6   The winner is the first player to reach No. 63. He must arrive by the exact score required. If he overshoots the mark, he must go up to 63 and move his counter backwards by the amount of the excess.

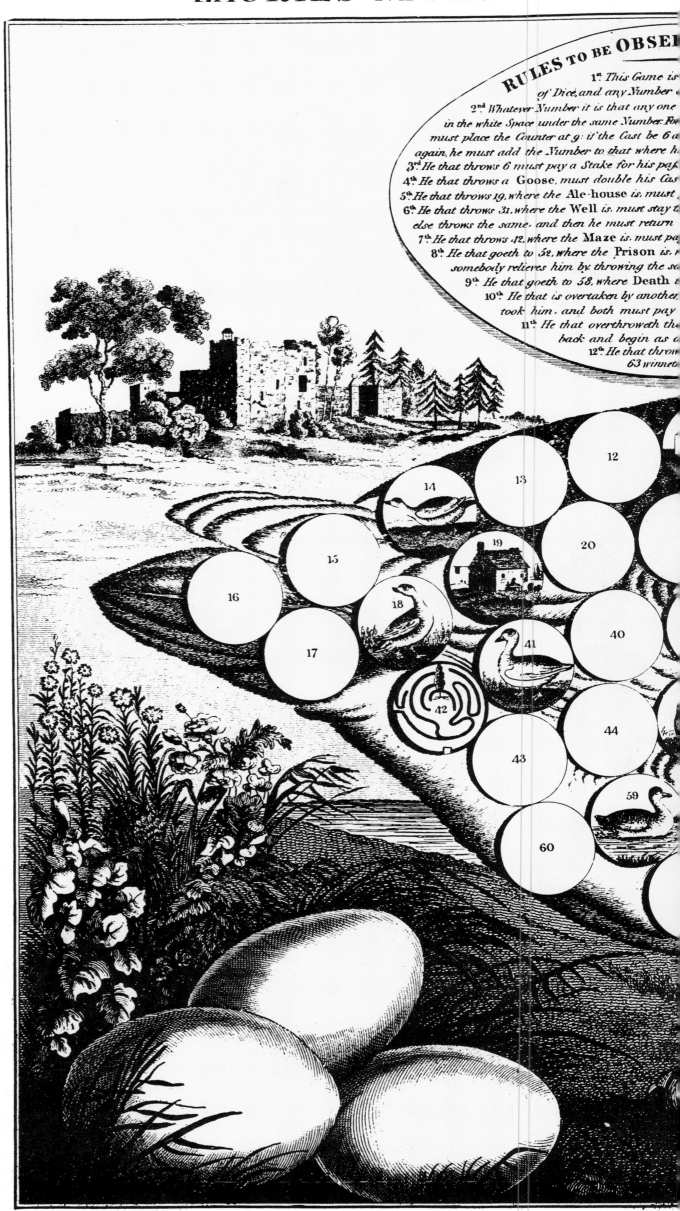

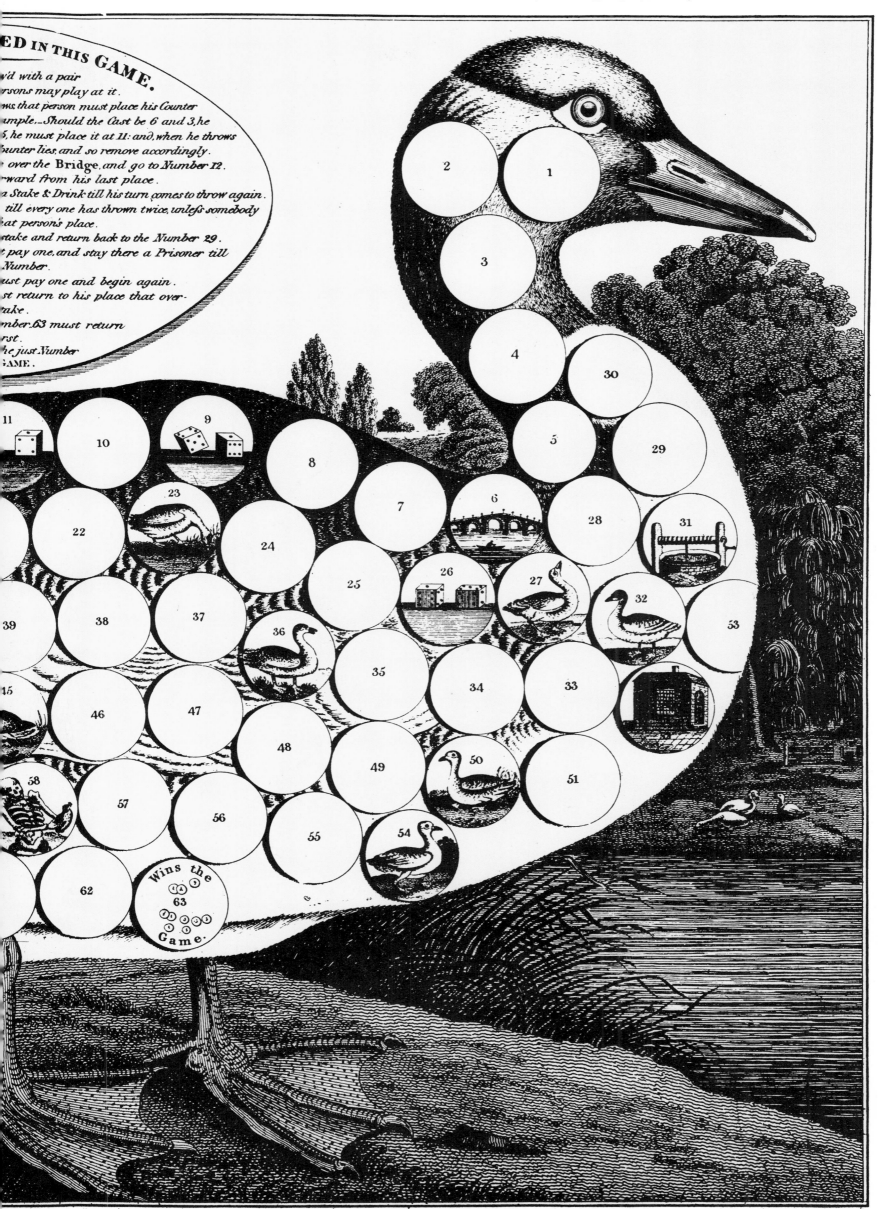

THE
NEW GAME OF
HUMAN LIFE

A 'moral' game, published in 1790 by John Wallis and E. Newbery, 'Human Life' is advertised as 'the most Agreeable & Rational Recreation ever invented for Youth of both Sexes'.
The publishers add: 'N.B. It is necessary to inform the Purchaser, the Totum must be marked with Figures 1, 2, 3, 4, 5, 6 to avoid introducing a Dice Box into private Families.'

The New Game
of
HUMAN LIFE,
with
RULES for PLAYING:
being
the most Agreeable & Rational Recreation
ever Invented for
Youth of both Sexes.

LONDON.
Published July 29, 1790, by J. Wallis
No. 16 Ludgate Street & E. Newbery
Corner of St Paul's Church
Yard
1790

CONCISE RULES

1 This is a game for any number of players. Each is provided with a counter of a different colour as an equal number of tokens (at least 12) with which to pay 'stakes'. Before play begins, each pays 4 tokens to the pool.

2 Players spin the totum to determine the order of play. The highest scorer goes first, the second highest next, and so on.

3 Beginning in the Age of Infancy to Youth, the players in turn spin the totum twice and advance by the total scored. Each age consists of 12 years, and players must not stop at any of these milestone years, viz. Nos. 12 (The Youth), 24 (The Young Man), 36 (The Prime of Life), 48 (The Sedate Man), 60 (The Old Man), or 72 (Decrepitude). Any player arriving on such a number must move forward again by the number of his score. If a player scored a pair of sixes at the start, he would by this system be carried straight through to 84 (The Immortal Man). To avoid this, players who begin with a pair of sixes go instead to 39 (The Historian).

4 In their passage through the 7 Ages, the players will encounter various hazards. These are described in detail on the gameboard, and are summarized here in numerical order:
No. 7. Take 1 token and go to 42.
No. 11. Pay 1 token and miss 2 turns.
No. 15. Take 2 tokens and go to 55.
No. 17. Take 1 token and go to 42.
No. 19. Pay 1 token and go to 38.
No. 22. Pay 2 tokens and go back to 3.
No. 26. Stay until displaced by another, then go to the latter's place.
No. 30. Pay 4 tokens and go back to 6.
No. 34. Take 2 tokens and go to 56.
No. 40. Pay 2 tokens and go back to 5.
No. 44. Pay 4 tokens and return to Start.
No. 52. Go to 78.
No. 58. Go to 82.
No. 63. Pay 2 tokens and go back to 2.
No. 68. Take 2 tokens and go to 80.
No. 71. Pay 2 tokens and go back to 16.
No. 74. Take 1 token and miss a turn.
No. 77. Pay 4 tokens and go back to 8.
Finally, the Tragic Author at 45 may go directly to the Immortal Man at 84, and win the game by succeeding him.

5 If a player arrives on a number already occupied, the 2 players change places. Any fines due at either place are paid by the intruding player.

6 The winner is the player who first reaches 84. Unless he travels via the route of the Tragic Author, described above, he must spin the exact amount required for Immortality. If he overshoots the mark, he must go back by as many places as he has exceeded it.

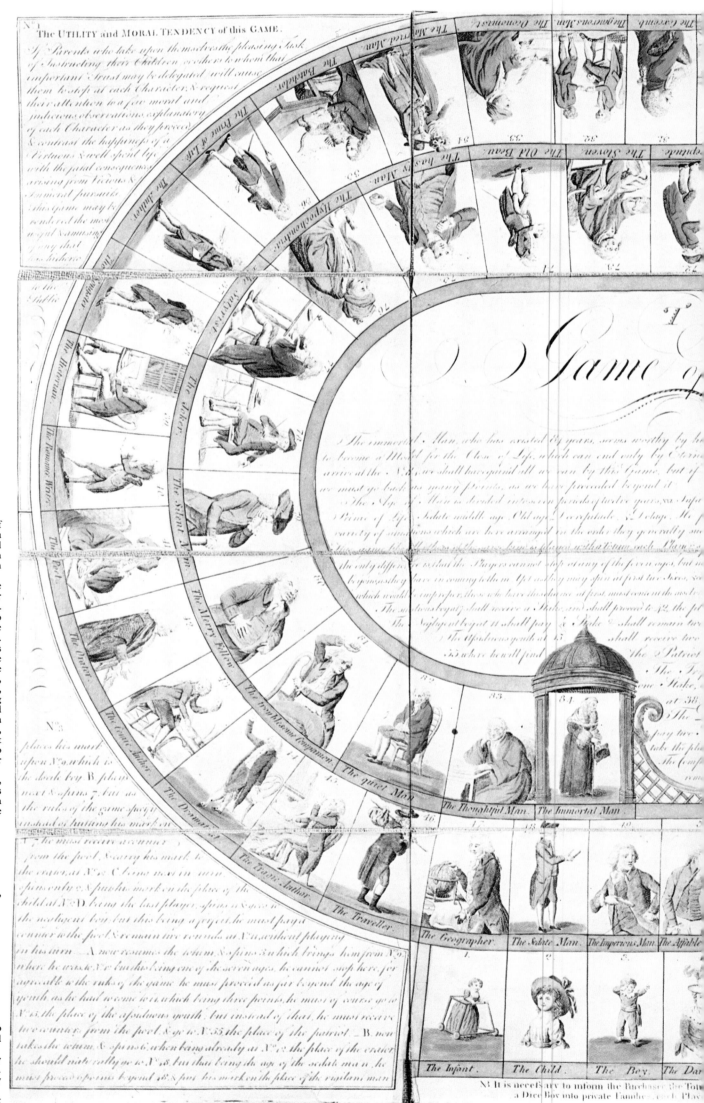

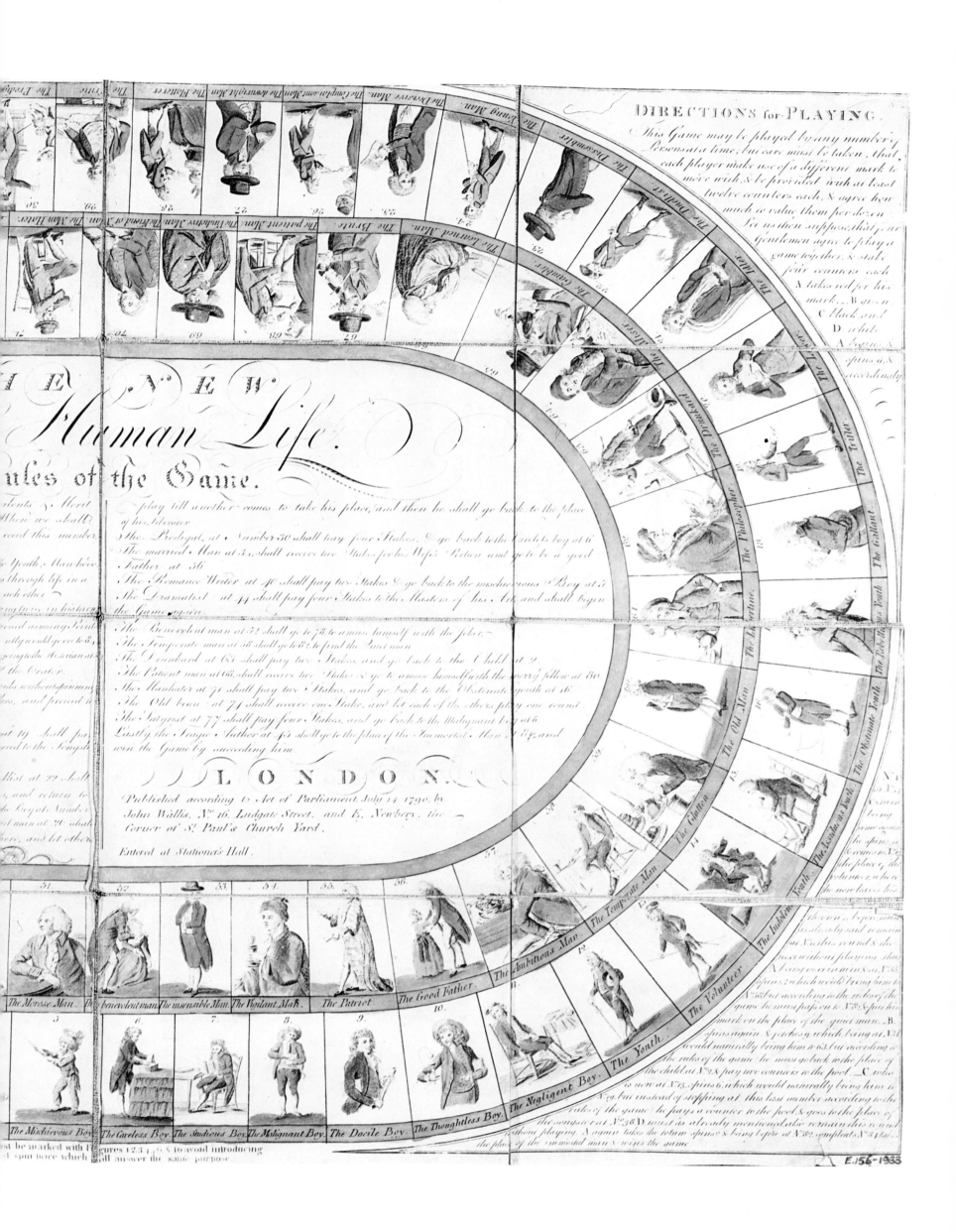

21

SNAKES
&
LADDERS 1

This is the earliest known 'Snakes & Ladders' game. It was registered in October 1892 by F.H. Ayres of London, and the example reproduced here is in the collection of the Bethnal Green Museum, London. Like many early board games, this circular 'Snakes & Ladders' requires the players to follow a spiral path to the winning number. The track is numbered from 1–100, and includes 5 Snakes descending and 5 Ladders ascending.

By the turn of the century 'Snakes & Ladders' had become enormously popular, and it is interesting to compare the design of this board with that of the more familiar rectangular game on pages 90–91.

1 This is a game for 2–6 players. Each is provided with a counter of a different colour.

2 The order of play is determined by throwing the die. The highest scorer begins, the second highest goes next, and so on.

3 The players throw the die in turn and advance by the number indicated. Players throwing a 6 are entitled to another turn (but not to a third throw if a second 6 is scored). Gradually the counters travel round the board, aiming for Square No. 100.

4 If a counter is played into a square from which a Ladder rises, it is carried up and placed in the square at the top of the Ladder. If it is played into a square occupied by the head of a Snake, it is carried down to the square at the end of the Snake's tail. Counters are played freely across squares bearing other parts of the Ladders and the Snakes; these are regarded as conventional squares.

5 If a counter is played into a square occupied by another player's counter, it must be returned to its previous square.

6 The winner is the player who first gets to Square No. 100. The exact number required must be cast, i.e. the 100 mark must not be overshot.

HARLEQUIN
OR LE NOUVEAU JEU D'ARLEQUIN

The comic-sad character of Harlequin, a favourite figure of intrigue in French and Italian light comedy, is here the master of ceremonies in a French dice game. The players throw 2 dice and occupy numbered circles according to their total score. If an opponent throws a similar total, he scoops up the first player's stake. If a 7 is thrown, Harlequin is the winner and the stake vanishes into, or, more strictly, is placed upon, the masked figure's sack. The winner is the last player left in the game, and he may then plunder Harlequin's sack of treasure and clear the board of all tokens remaining there. This version of the game was produced in a two-language edition, the rules being printed beneath the gameboard in Dutch and French.

N. 72.

Het nieuw Arlequin Spel.

Le nouveau Jeu d'Arlequin.

24

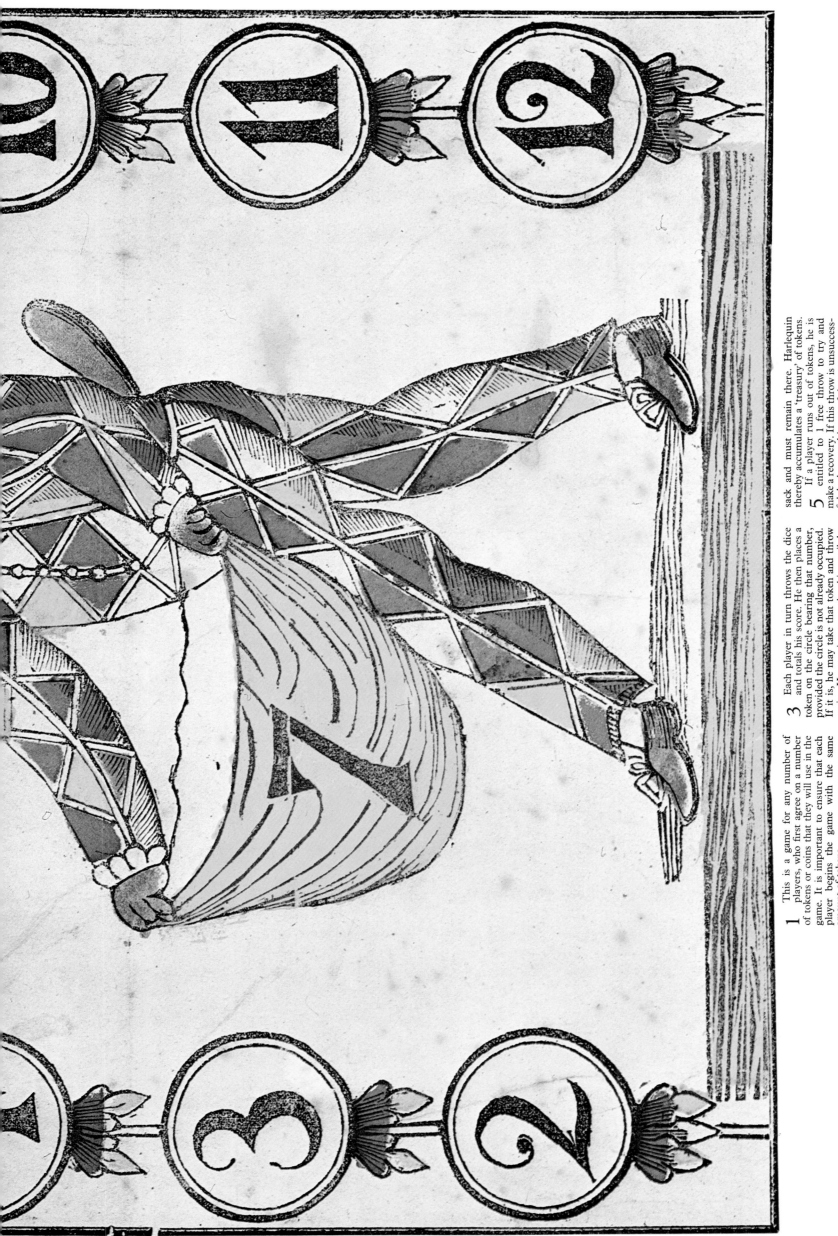

1   This is a game for any number of players, who first agree on a number of tokens or coins that they will use in the game. It is important to ensure that each player begins the game with the same amount of tokens.

2   The order of play is determined by throwing 2 dice. The player with the highest total begins, the second highest goes next, and so on.

3   Each player in turn throws the dice and totals his score. He then places a token on the circle bearing that number, provided the circle is not already occupied. If it is, he may take that token and throw again. He continues to do this until he throws the number of an empty circle, on which he places his own token.

4   If a player scores 7, then Harlequin is the winner. The token is put into his sack and must remain there. Harlequin thereby accumulates a 'treasury' of tokens.

5   If a player runs out of tokens, he is entitled to 1 free throw to try and make a recovery. If this throw is unsuccessful, he loses and is out of the game.

6   The winner is the last player remaining in the game. He is entitled to all Harlequin's treasure and to all the tokens resting on other numbers.

WALLIS'S NEW GAME OF UNIVERSAL HISTORY AND CHRONOLOGY

This chronologically organized romp through history was published in London on 20 May 1814 by John Wallis of 42 Skinner Street, Snow Hill.

In addition to the gameboard, Mr Wallis's customers received a 34-page book of rules which guided them through the 'Chronology of the most remarkable Events from the Creation to the present Time'.

Not all the panels on the gameboard contain an illustration. A number convey their message in words, and of these 16 are what we have referred to in the rules below as 'History numbers'. The original idea was that if, for example, a player arrived on No. 5, he would look up that number in the book of rules and be referred to the 'Outlines of History' section at the back of the book, where half a page of information about the subject of Panel 5 awaited him. For reasons of space we have limited ourselves to observing the original ruling for a player arriving on such 'History numbers', viz. that 'he shall have the privilege . . . of spinning again, and be rewarded with a counter from each player'.

1 This is a game for up to 12 players. The 12 counters marked A–L are placed on the table face down, and each player in turn draws 1 of these. Whoever picks the earliest letter in the alphabet spins first, and the others follow in rotation. Each player is also provided with an equal number of tokens for paying fines, etc., and before the start of the game places 6 in the pool.

2 The players spin the totum in turn and advance by the number indicated.

If a player arrives on a number already occupied, he must return to his former place and receive 2 tokens from the other player for so doing.

3 The fines and directions associated with particular numbers are only to be paid or observed if a player has arrived there by spinning, not if he was sent there from another number.

4 If a player arrives on a 'History number', he is entitled to spin again. The various 'active' numbers and their directions are summarized below. It is assumed that any player arriving on a number to which tokens have been paid, has the right to collect any remaining there. (Wallis's original spellings of proper names have been preserved.)

No. 3. Universal Deluge. Begin again.

No. 4. Building of Babel. Pay 6 tokens to the pool.

No. 5. History number (Babylonish and Assyrian monarchies founded). Spin again, and receive 1 token from each player.

No. 6. History number (Kingdom of Egypt). Spin again, and receive 1 token from each player.

No. 7. History number (founding of Kingdom of Sicyon). Spin again, and receive 1 token from each player.

No. 8. Letters invented by Memnon, an Egyptian. Receive 2 tokens from each player.

No. 10. History number (birth of Moses). Spin again, and receive 1 token from each player.

No. 11. Kingdom of Athens founded. Pay 3 tokens to Rome, your more successful rival (No. 18).

No. 13. History number (Trojan War).

Spin again, and receive 1 token from each player.

No. 15. The 10 tribes of Jews revolt. Pay 4 tokens to the pool.

No. 16. Homer flourished. If you can say who he was, and what he wrote, receive 2 tokens from each player; if not, pay 6 to the pool.

No. 18. History number (Rome founded). Spin again, and receive 1 token from each player.

No. 22. Public library founded in Athens. Spin again.

No. 25. Socrates, the greatest heathen philosopher, condemned to die by poison in his 70th year. Miss 1 turn to lament the ingratitude of his countrymen.

No. 42. Jerusalem destroyed by the Romans. Place 3 tokens on No. 35.

No. 43. Eruption of Vesuvius overwhelms the cities of Herculanæum and Pompeii. Go on to No. 119.

No. 44. End of second Jewish war. Pay 4 tokens to No. 18.

No. 45. Title of Pope bestowed on first bishop of Rome. Go to No. 60.

No. 49. History number (Kingdom of Caledonia, or Scotland, revives under Fergus). Spin again, and receive 1 token from each player.

No. 50. History number (Pharamond becomes first king of France). Spin again, and receive 1 token from each player.

No. 51. History number (Romans evacuate Britain). Spin again, and receive 1 token from each player.

No. 53. Commencement of the Heptarchy, or Seven Kingdoms of the Saxons in England. Go to No. 66.

No. 57. Dreadful plague sweeps all over Europe, Asia, and Africa. Miss 1 turn to deplore this calamity.

No. 58. History number (Mahomet born). Spin again, and receive 1 token from each player.

No. 68. The Picts totally defeated by the Scots; both kingdoms are united under Kenneth. Pay 4 tokens to the conquerors at No. 49.

No. 69. The navy of England first established by Alfred. Spin again.

No. 72. Pope Boniface VII deposed and banished from Rome for his crimes. Go back to No. 45.

No. 74. Great massacre of the Danes in England. Pay 3 to Alfred, at No. 70.

No. 76. Battle of Hastings. Say who was slain here, or pay 6 to the pool.

No. 78. First Crusade. Pay 4 to the pool for its ill success.

No. 81. Ireland conquered by Henry II. Pay 3 to No. 51.

No. 83. Kings of France and England show their submission to Pope Alexander III by holding the stirrups while he mounts his horse. Place 4 tokens on No. 60.

No. 85. King John compelled by his barons to sign Magna Charta. Spin again.

No. 86. History number (Empire of the House of Austria begins in Germany). Spin again, and receive 1 token from each player.

No. 88. Edward I defeats Llewellyn, Prince of Wales, and unites that country to England. Pay 3 to No. 51.

No. 89. History number (Commencement of the Turkish Empire in Bythinia, under Othman). Spin again, and receive 1 token from each player.

No. 91. Establishment of the Helvetian Confederacy, or Republic of Switzerland. Pay 2 to No. 86 since, before this, it formed part of the dominions of Germany.

No. 96. John Wickliffe exposes the errors of the Romish Church. Spin again.

No. 97. The art of printing invented by John Guttenburg. Take 6 from the pool.

No. 98. One hundred thousand people drowned by an irruption of the sea at Dort, in Holland. Miss 1 turn to lament this catastrophe.

No. 100. History number (Moors expelled from Spain). Spin again, and receive 1 token from each player.

No. 104. History number (Revolution in Sweden under Gustavus Vasa). Spin again, and receive 1 token from each player.

No. 106. Dissolution of religious houses in England. Reward Wickliffe, at No. 96, with 3 tokens.

No. 107. William Shakespeare born. Receive 1 token from each player to reward his genius.

No. 108. Massacre of St Bartholomew in Paris. Miss 1 turn.

No. 110. Destruction of the Spanish Armada. Give some account of this, or pay 3 to the pool.

No. 112. Sixty-eight thousand persons destroyed by the plague in London. Miss 2 turns.

No. 113. The Great Fire of London, which continued 3 days and consumed 13,000 houses. Miss 1 turn.

No. 115. History number (Prussia becomes a kingdom). Spin again, and receive 1 token from each player.

No. 116. History number (Russian empire is civilized by Peter the Great). Spin again, and receive 1 token from each player.

No. 121. Accession of George III to the throne of England. Spin again.

No. 124. War between Great Britain and America. Pay 3 to the pool.

No. 125. Death of Captain Cooke at Owhyee (Hawaii). Stop 1 turn to lament this great man.

No. 129. The King and Queen of France beheaded by the guillotine. Pay 3 tokens to No. 50.

No. 134. Bonaparte crowned Emperor of the French by the Pope. Pay 4 to No. 129.

No. 138. His Royal Highness George Prince of Wales created Regent of the British Empire. You are appointed First Lord of the Treasury. Therefore take possession of the pool, and all the counters remaining on the board, and proclaim the game at an end.

No. 27. Alexander the Great flourished. Pay 2 tokens to the pool unless you know who he was.

No. 28. Death of Darius Codomannus, last king of Persia. Pay 4 tokens to his conqueror, at No. 27.

No. 30. Carthage falls to Romans. Pay 2 tokens to No. 18.

No. 31. Civil war in Rome, between Sylla and Marius. Pay 3 tokens to No. 18.

No. 33. Julius Caesar assassinated. Miss 1 turn.

No. 35. Jesus Christ, the Messiah, born. Universal peace prevails. Take half the pool and spin again.

No. 37. The crucifixion and resurrection of our Lord. Miss 2 turns to lament his sufferings, and receive 3 tokens from each player for the blessings derived from them.

No. 41. Rome set on fire by Nero. Miss 2 turns.

THE BLUE BIRD

Produced in 1913 by the Chad Valley company of Harborne, England, this simple and charming children's game was inspired by Maurice Maeterlinck's allegory L'oiseau bleu, which first appeared in 1909. In this adapted version the players move from scene to scene until finally the Blue Bird, and happiness, are attained by the winner.

1 This is a game for 2–4 young children. Each is provided with a counter of a different colour, and places it below Circle 1 in the centre of the gameboard. Twenty Blue Bird tokens are placed in a line above the gameboard. Each player then draws 2 Blue Bird tokens from this pool.

2 The order of play is determined by spinning the totum. The Blue Bird counts highest, then 3, 2 and 1. The player with the highest score begins.

3 The players in turn spin the totum and advance by the number indicated. Once a player has reached Circle 1 or farther, he or she may collect a Blue Bird from the pool each time it turns up on the totum. But if a player has yet to reach Circle 1, then he or she cannot claim a Blue Bird and must wait until the next chance to spin.

4 The players move their counters round the board, aiming for 10 (Home Again). If, on the way, a player lands on 3 or 6, he or she may take 1 Blue Bird from the pool. But if a player lands on 9 (The Palace of Night), he or she must give back 1 Blue Bird to the pool.

5 The game ends when the first player arrives on 10. To do so, the exact number should be thrown. If, however, a player overshoots by 1, he or she may go to Light – and from there on to Home. But if a player overshoots by 2, he or she must go to Night – and from there back to 4. The first player to reach 10 may take 3 Blue Birds.

6 The winner is the player with the most Blue Birds.

THE NEW GAME OF VIRTUE REWARDED AND VICE PUNISHED

In this early 19th-century spiral race game there is no respite for the players in the form of hazard-free spaces. Every number, from the House of Correction at No. 1 to the winning post at Virtue (No. 33), holds out punishment or reward for the player alighting there. Faith, Impertinence, Truth, Sloth . . . the judgments alternate between favourable and unfavourable, with Hope (No. 14) rather unsettlingly neutral ('Wait with patience until the next turn').

The game was devised by T. Newton and was published in 1818 in London by Wm. Darton of 58 Holborn Hill. The gameboard is a hand-coloured engraving mounted in 12 sections on linen and contained in a slipcase.

An 8-page book of rules accompanied the game. This declares that the game 'is designed with a view to promoting progressive Improvement of the Juvenile Mind, and to deter them from pursuing the dangerous Paths of Vice'.

London Published by W. Darton, 58, Holborn Hill.

By T. NEWTON, Inventor of the MANSION.
NEW GAME of the MANSION

1 This is a game for 2–12 players. Each is provided with a counter of a different colour and 12 tokens, 4 of which are placed initially in the pool.

2 The order of play is established by drawing lots. Players then spin the totum in turn and advance by the number indicated.

3 After arriving on a number, players must carry out the directions given. But if a player is sent to another number, he must not also carry out the directions applying there.

4 The aim of each player is to attain Virtue (No. 33). The directions that he or she may meet en route are as follows.

No. 1. House of Correction. Miss 3 turns.
No. 2. Prudence. Spin again.
No. 3. Hypocrisy. Pay 2 tokens to the pool and 1 to each player.
No. 4. Honesty. Receive 1 token from each player.
No. 5. Folly. Pay 2 to the pool and spin again.
No. 6. Charity. Take 2 more spins.
No. 7. Avarice. Forfeit half your tokens to the pool.
No. 8. Poverty. Receive 2 relieving tokens from the pool.
No. 9. The Stocks. Wait here and miss 2 turns.
No. 10. Faith. Receive 1 token from each player.
No. 11. Impertinence. Go back to Prudence to learn good manners.
No. 12. Truth. Receive 4 tokens from the pool and 1 from each player.
No. 13. Sloth. Go back to the House of Correction and miss 2 turns.
No. 14. Hope. Wait with patience until the next turn.
No. 15. Luxury. Pay 1 token into the pool and 1 to each player.
No. 16. Friendship. Spin again.
No. 17. Carelessness. Go back to Prudence.
No. 18. Patience. Claim 3 tokens from the pool.
No. 19. Brutality. You must be sent to the House of Correction.
No. 20. Morality. Receive 1 token from each player.
No. 21. Malice. Pay 1 token to each player and 1 to the pool.
No. 22. Modesty. Spin again.
No. 23. Contention. Forfeit 1 token to each player and spin again.
No. 24. Piety. Advance to Temperance.
No. 25. Envy. Miss 2 turns.
No. 26. Confusion. Go back to your former place.
No. 27. Diligence. Receive 1 token from each player and spin again.
No. 28. Obstinacy. Go back to Patience and pay 2 tokens to the pool.
No. 29. Civility. Advance 2 places.
No. 30. Falsehood. You are put in the Stocks and miss 3 turns.
No. 31. Temperance. Spin again.
No. 32. Anger. Go back to Patience and miss 2 turns.
No. 33. Virtue. You win the game and claim the contents of the pool.

5 The winner is the first player to arrive exactly on Virtue (No. 33). Any player overshooting must return to his former place and wait his turn.

LUDO
OR PARCHEESI

'Parcheesi' or 'Parchisi' (from the Hindi word <u>pachis</u>, meaning '25') was modified and introduced into England as 'Ludo' in about 1880.

According to F.R.B. Whitehouse, the author of <u>Table Games of Georgian and Victorian Days</u> (London, 1951), the game was played at the court of the Mogul Emperor Akbar (1542–1605). In his enthusiasm the Emperor had one of his courtyards paved in marble in the design of the board. He and his courtiers then played the game, using as 'pieces' 16 girls from the harem.

The 'Ludo' board game illustrated here was published by Chad Valley in 1905.

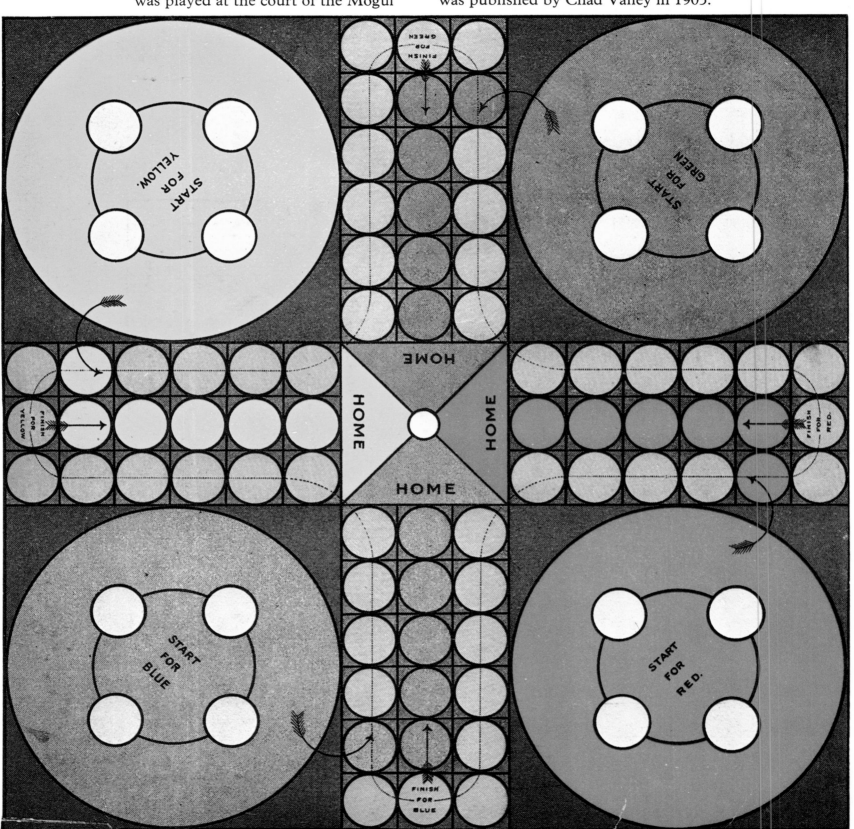

1   This is a game for 2, 3 or 4 players. Each takes 4 counters of the same colour, and places them in the appropriate Starting Enclosure.

2   Players throw the die in turn. A 6 is needed to start, and the successful player then moves 1 counter into the first circle of the track indicated by the arrow. He or she then has another throw, and moves the counter forward by the corresponding number of spaces.

3   At each subsequent throw of a 6, a player may either bring a fresh counter into play, or advance a counter already on the track. A 6 on the first throw always entitles the player to a second turn, but not subsequently, i.e. a third turn is not allowed if another 6 is thrown on the second turn.

4   When a counter is played into a space occupied by an opponent, it takes its place. The displaced counter is returned to its Starting Enclosure, from which it is again started in the usual way.

5   When 2 or more counters of the same colour are played into the same space, 1 is placed on top of the other and together they form a Barrier, which no other counter may seize or pass over. If a Barrier prevents a counter being advanced its full number of spaces, that turn is lost.

6   After a counter has been round the outside track and comes back to its own colour, it is played up the centre line of spaces to Home. Here the exact number required must be cast, i.e. the Home mark may not be overshot.

7   The winner is the player who first gets all 4 counters Home.

ROYAL LUDO

This modification of 'Ludo' was patented in 1891 by Alfred Collier, a games manufacturer from Hackney in London. The original dice were marked, in addition to the spots, with a 'Prince of Wales Feathers' and a 'Crown' device on 2 of the faces; the board is similarly marked with 'Feather' and 'Crown' spaces.

In March 1905 Alfred Collier patented and marketed another design, called 'Monarch Ludo', that combined the principles of 'Ludo' and 'Royal Ludo'. The board has an additional outer track, the 4 corners of which are known as 'Monarch Corners' and are illustrated with portraits of King Edward VII.

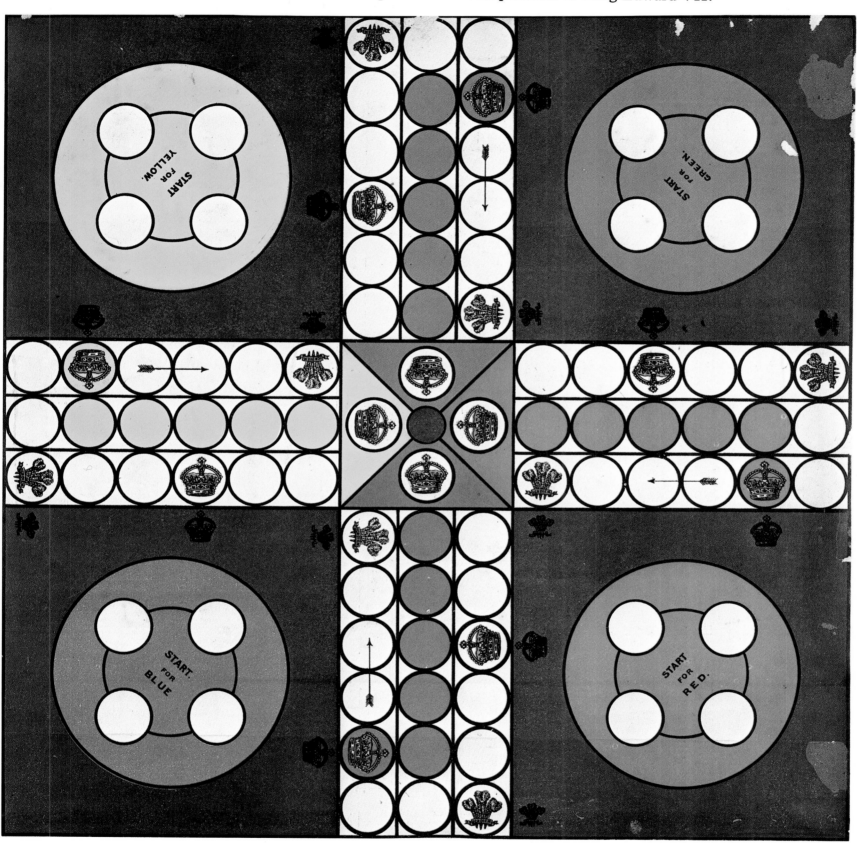

1 This is a game for 2, 3 or 4 players. Each takes 4 counters of the same colour, and places them in the appropriate Starting Enclosure.

2 Players throw the die in turn. A Crown throw (represented by a 6) is needed to start, and the successful player then moves 1 counter into the Crown space beside his or her Enclosure. The player then has another throw, and moves the counter forward by the corresponding number of spaces along the outside track indicated by the arrow.

3 At each subsequent Crown throw (of a 6), a player may either bring a fresh counter into play, or advance a counter already on the track into the next Crown space. If he is unable to make either of these moves, he loses that turn.

4 A Crown move enables a counter to be advanced over any number of

spaces including Feather spaces, and always entitles the player to a second turn – but not to subsequent turns, i.e. a third turn is not allowed if another Crown or 6 is thrown on the second turn.

5 A player throwing a Feather (represented by a 5) advances one of his counters into the next Feather space, but he may never move over a Crown space to do so.

6 When a counter is played into a space occupied by an opponent, the player may either return the opponent's counter to its Starting Enclosure, or place his counter on top of it to form a Double. The opponent may then carry the Double forward at every possible turn, i.e. he cannot opt to move any of his other counters. The player owning the top half of a Double may jump his counter forward on its own when it is his turn to move.

7 A player may not advance a counter into a space occupied by another of his own colour. He may not play a Double into a space occupied by any other counter, or counters in the case of another Double. In all such cases, if he is unable to make another move, he loses that turn. Unless prevented, a player must always move by the full amount of his score whether to his advantage or not.

8 After a counter has been round the outside track and comes back to its own colour, it is played up the centre line of spaces to Home. This can be reached only by throwing a Crown or 6.

9 If a counter forming the upper half of a Double is carried past its Home colour, that piece has to be played right round the board again.

10 The winner is the player who first gets all 4 counters Home.

GAME OF THE GOOD CHILDREN OR JEU DES BONS ENFANS

This spiral race game takes a mocking view of marriage for its theme. If a man (all players are here presumed male) arrives at the marriage space (No. 9) with his first throw, he is rewarded for his impetuosity by being immediately cuckolded. The pattern of the dice throw

determines whether he shall be happy about this, and move to No. 29, or unhappy, and take up residence at No. 42. No married man may be released from

this prison-like state unless someone else arrives on his number and takes his place. When this happens, the husband's liberation is made to coincide with the

death of his wife, for he then proceeds directly to her burial, at No. 58, where he pays 1 token for the gravedigger's services and continues his road towards the amply provisioned table at No. 63, where all the Good Children (presumably God's) are seen tucking in together.

34

1   This is a game for any number of players, each of whom is provided with a stock of tokens and a coloured counter. The counter is placed beside Square No. 1.

2   The order of play is determined by throwing the dice. The highest scorer begins, the second highest goes next, and so on.

3   The players throw the dice in turn and advance by the total indicated. Players do not stop on picture squares por-

traying Old Women (D. Allix, D. Lorance, etc.), but advance again by the number scored.

4   Anyone arriving on No. 6 (The Serenade) must pay the musicians.

5   Anyone who on his first throw scores 9 (The Wedding) with a 5 and 4 must pay 1 token to the pool for his wedding and move to the place of the Happy Cuckold (No. 29). He may only be released from here

by someone arriving on the same square, who takes his place. He then proceeds to his wife's burial (No. 58), pays the grave-digger (1 token to the pool) and carries on from there.

6   Anyone who on his first throw scores 9 with a 3 and 6 must pay 1 token for his wedding and move to the place of the Unhappy Cuckold (No. 42). He too may only be released by someone arriving on the same square, who takes his place. He then proceeds as described in Rule 5.

7   If a player arrives at No. 9 (The Wedding) by some other combination of scores, he spits in the bowl and must return to the Start.

8   If a player stops at No. 19 (The Woman in Labour), he must pay tribute, or 1 token to the pool.

9   If a player stops at No. 29, and finds it vacant, he must pay tribute or 1 token to the pool, and miss a turn.

10   He who stops at No. 42, and finds it vacant, receives tribute (1 token) and continues on his way.

11   He who stops at No. 52 (The Baptism) must be a godparent, pay 1 token for the expenses and return to No. 30.

12   Anyone arriving at No. 58 (The Burial) must make an offering of 1 token and return to the Start.

13   The winner is the first player to arrive at No. 63 (Table of the Good Children). He takes the pool. It is not essential to score the exact number to finish, i.e. over-shooting is permitted.

A Paris chez Jacques Chereau Rue St Jacques aux 2 Colonnes N.º 257.

A Paris   rue St Jaque   aux Privilege du Roy

A Paris Chez

35

THE ROYAL PASTIME OF CUPID OR ENTERTAINING GAME OF THE SNAKE

This 18th-century game is similar in appearance to traditional games of 'Goose'. The track contains 63 numbered circles, and several of the hazards are similar, though placed on different numbers. For example, the Bridge, Fountain, Labyrinth, Wood, and Coffin of this game have as their equivalents in the 'Golden Goose' game on pages 18–19 the Bridge, Well, Maze, Prison, and Death. Board games of this vintage are now very rare since they were not originally mounted on linen, as later games were, and few have survived. This example is based on a design by John Garrett and was 'Printed and sould . . . at his Shop, next ye stayers of ye Royall Exchange in Cornhill'. In the 19th century it was published by R.H. Laurie of 53 Fleet Street, London.

1 This is a game for 2–6 players. Each is provided with a counter of a different colour, which he or she places near the head of the Snake, and with an equal supply of tokens. An agreed number, say 3, is paid to the pool.

2 The order of play is determined by throwing the dice. The player with the highest number starts, the second highest goes next, and so on.

3 Players throw the dice in turn and advance by the total indicated. If in the first round a player throws a 7, he must move as follows: if the 7 is composed of 1 and 6, he goes forward to 16; if of 2 and 5, to 25, and if of 4 and 3, to 43.

4 Around the spiral of the Snake are certain other hazards. No player may rest on a plain Cupid space, but must go forward again by as many as he threw before. If a player arrives on 5 (The Bridge), he must pay a toll equal to the number of tokens he placed in the pool, and advance to 12 (Chair), where he must rest and miss a turn. If he arrives on 18, he must pay beverage to Cupid (1 token), and miss 2 turns unless another player releases him sooner by also arriving on 18, in which case they change places. If he arrives on 30 (Fountain), he must wash himself there until another player releases him, in which case they change places, as for 18. If he arrives on 38, he must feast with Cupid, pay a fine equal to his original stake, e.g. 3 tokens, and miss a turn. If he arrives on 46 (Labyrinth), he must go back to 23, and resume from there next time round. If he arrives on 54 (Wood), he is trapped in the net until freed by another player taking his place; he returns to that player's place, and pays a ransom of 2 tokens. If he arrives on 59 (Coffin), he must pay 1 token for the grave and return to the Start.

5 Players arriving on spaces occupied by other players take their place. The displaced player goes back to the other's old position and pays a fine of 1 token.

6 The winner is the player who first reaches the Delightful Garden of Cupid (No. 63). The exact number required must be cast, with no overshooting. If a player throws too high a number, he must count up to 63 and move backwards by the amount of the excess.

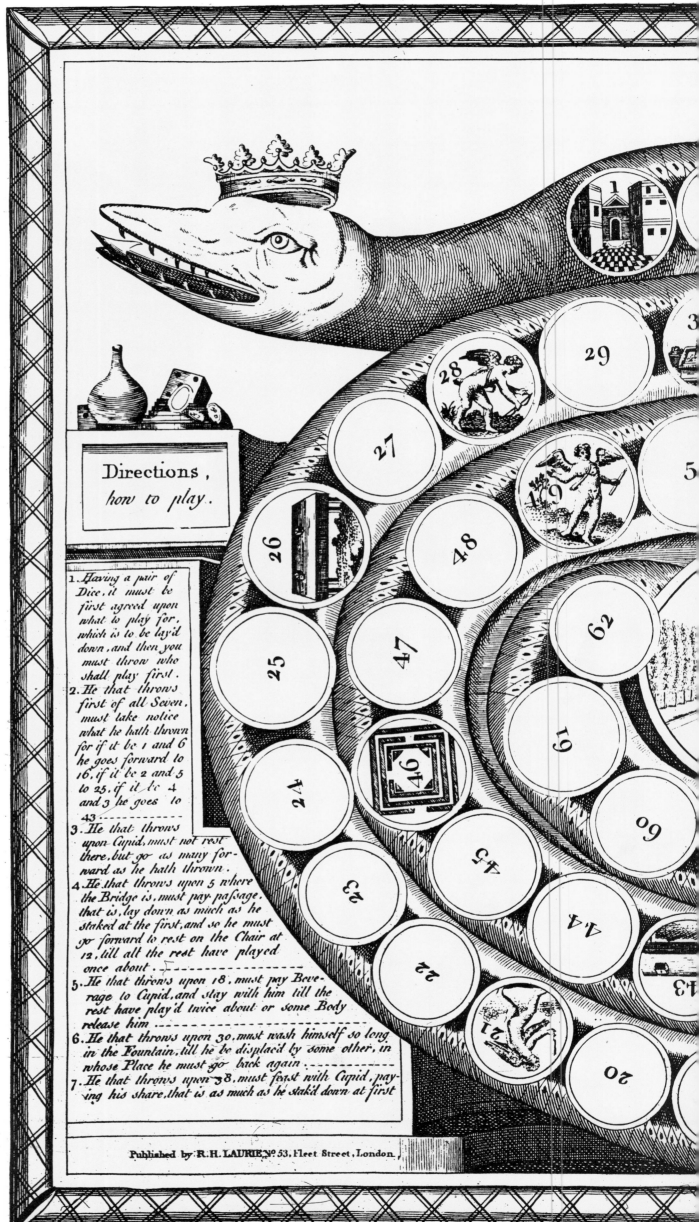

Directions, how to play.

1. Having a pair of Dice, it must be first agreed upon what to play for, which is to be lay'd down, and then you must throw who shall play first.

2. He that throws first of all Seven, must take notice what he hath thrown for if it be 1 and 6 he goes forward to 16, if it be 2 and 5 to 25, if it be 4 and 3 he goes to 43 — — — — —

3. He that throws upon Cupid, must not rest there, but go as many forward as he hath thrown.

4. He that throws upon 5 where the Bridge is, must pay passage, that is, lay down as much as he staked at the first, and so he must go forward to rest on the Chair at 12, till all the rest have played once about. — — — — —

5. He that throws upon 18, must pay Beverage to Cupid, and stay with him till the rest have play'd twice about or some Body release him — — — — —

6. He that throws upon 30, must wash himself so long in the Fountain, till he be displac'd by some other, in whose Place he must go back again — — — — —

7. He that throws upon 38, must feast with Cupid, paying his share, that is as much as he stakd down at first

Published by R.H. LAURIE, N⁰ 53, Fleet Street, London.

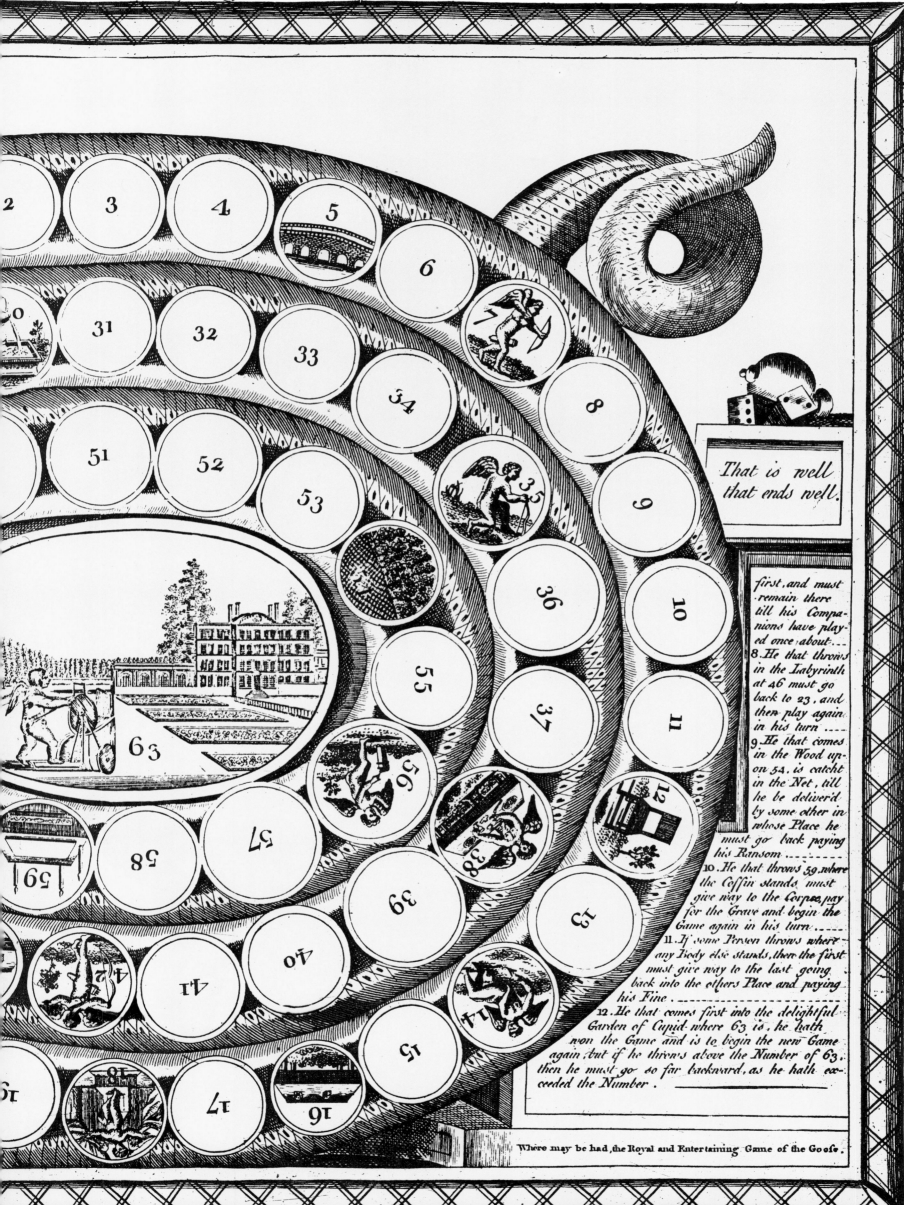

That is well
that ends well.

first, and must
remain there
till his Compa-
nions have play-
ed once about.
8. He that throws
in the Labyrinth
at 46 must go
back to 23, and
then play again
in his turn.
9. He that comes
in the Wood up-
on 54. is catcht
in the Net, till
he be deliver'd
by some other in
whose Place he
must go back paying
his Ransom.
10. He that throws 59. where
the Coffin stands must
give way to the Corpse, pay
for the Grave and begin the
Game again in his turn.
11. If some Person throws where
any Body else stands, then the first
must give way to the last, going
back into the others Place and paying
his Fine.
12. He that comes first into the delightful
Garden of Cupid. where 63 is, he hath
won the Game and is to begin the new Game
again. But if he throws above the Number of 63.
then he must go so far backward, as he hath exceeded the Number.

THE TAILLESS DONKEY

This game was published by Chad Valley in 1903. It was, and remains, a firm favourite at children's parties.

Before play began, the donkey was either placed flat on a table or pinned to a wall. Several loose tails were provided, which the blindfolded players endeavoured to fix in the correct position and so score maximum points. Editions of the game were offered in 2 qualities, at sixpence and 1 shilling, and special export editions were sent to France, where the game was also well received.

Another Chad Valley game, called 'Jonto or Dressing John Bull' (1905) follows a similar pattern of play. The gameboard, featuring a large printed figure of John Bull, was first hung on a wall. The players were then blindfolded in turn and provided with John Bull hats, buttonholes, etc., which they attempted to place in the correct positions, scoring points according to the accuracy of each placing.

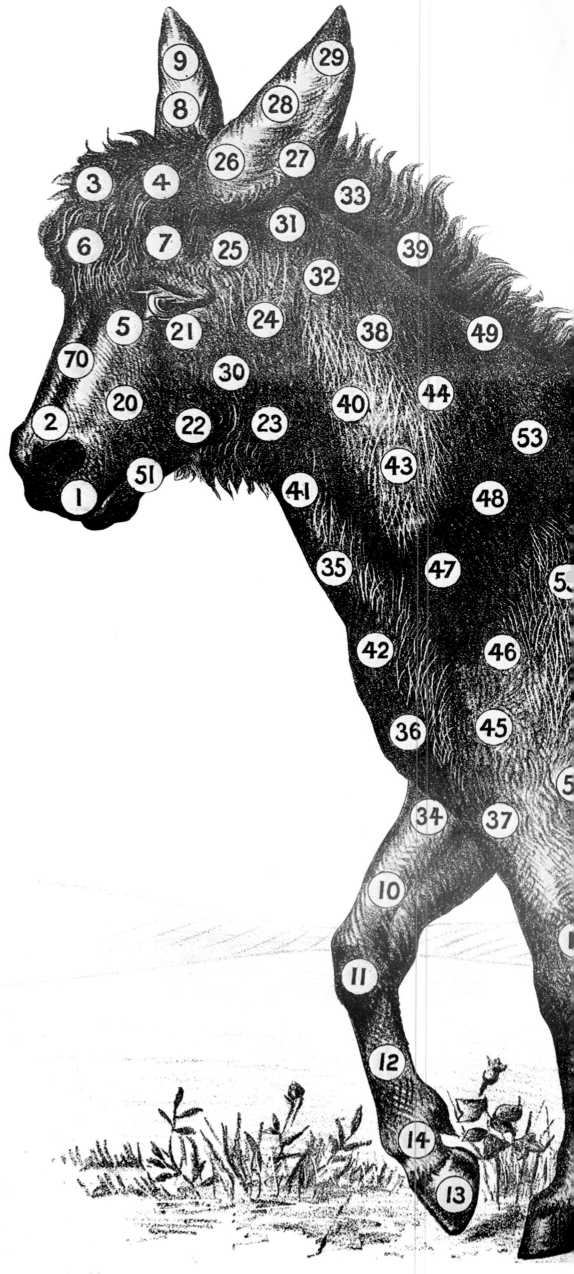

1   This is a game for any number of players. The book is placed flat on a table, and each player is in turn blindfolded while facing the picture at some distance from it, say about 4 feet (1.20 m). It is advisable to appoint an Umpire before play begins. He or she blindfolds the players, records the scores, and settles all disputes.

2   The player is then given the tail (from which the hole in the top end has been cut out), and after turning round three times he walks towards the picture and places the tail in what he thinks is the correct position.

3   The player scores according to the number of a circle showing through the hole in the top end of the tail. A score is made if the hole merely touches part of a circle. If no circle is touched, the player fails to score. A player attaching the tail to any of the following numbers loses 5 from his score: 1, 9, 11, 13, 17, 19, 21, 29, 50, 59. If the top end of the tail misses the Donkey entirely, the player loses 10 from his score.

4   The winner is the player with the highest score after an agreed number of turns.

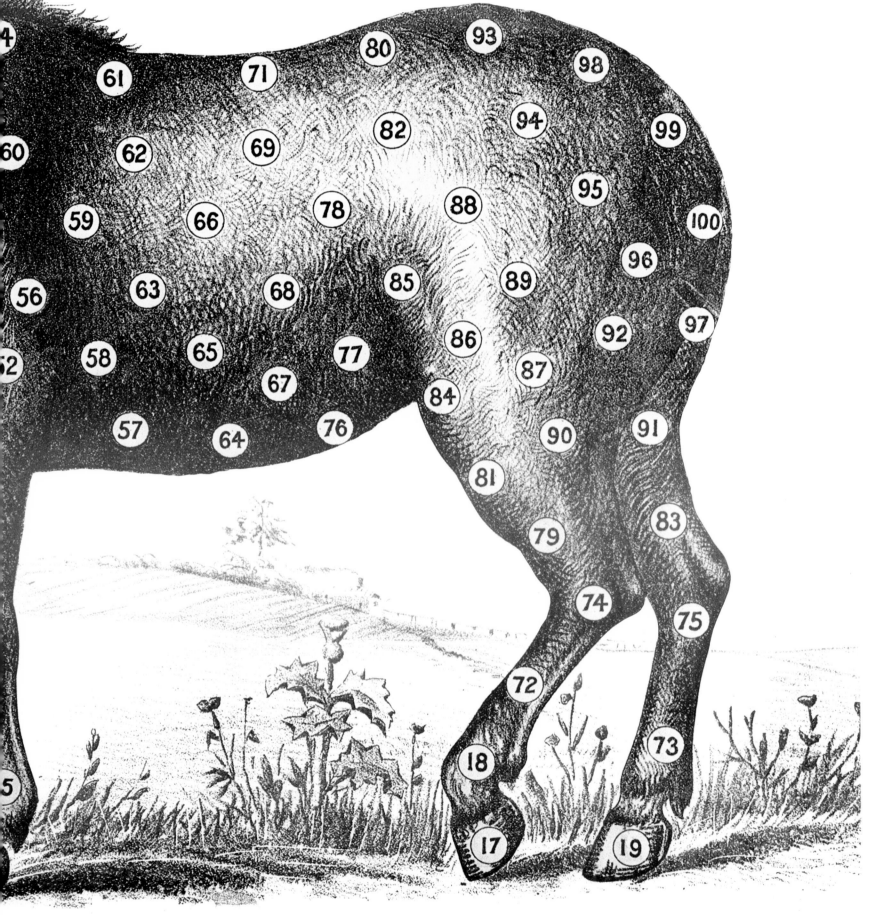

FRENCH REVOLUTION
OR
JEU DE LA RÉVOLUTION FRANÇAISE

The French were relatively quick to recognize the value of games for instructional and propaganda purposes. The Jeu de la Révolution Française, produced in 1791 at the height of the Revolution's success, adapts the traditional forms of the game of 'Goose' to political ends.

The players advance from the fall of the Bastille towards the National Assembly, or Palladium of Liberty. On the way, feudal rights are suppressed, Church property is seized, and the 'death's head' at No. 58 marks the execution of Foulon and Berthier, who were Black Market profiteers, and serves as a warning to others.

1   This is a game for any number of players, who first agree on the number of tokens that they will use in the game, and how much they will pay into the pool for the various levies recorded below. (For the sake of simplicity we will assume in these rules that the 'price' per incident is 1 token, but players may wish to introduce their own refinements.) At all events each player should begin with the same number of tokens. Each player is also provided with a coloured counter to mark his or her progress.

2   The order of play is determined by throwing the dice. The player with the highest total begins, the second highest goes next, and so on.

3   Each player throws the dice in turn and advances his or her counter by the total scored. Players may not set foot on the Bridled Geese: anyone arriving on a number occupied by Geese must move forward again by the amount shown on the dice until he is free of the Geese; i.e. if he again encounters Geese, he must again move on by the same method. Since the Geese are spaced at intervals of 9 squares, anyone having thrown a 9 would ordinarily be carried straight to No. 63 by this procedure. To avoid this, players throwing a 9 initially must move as follows: if the 9 is composed of 6 and 3, the player moves to No. 26; if it is composed of 5 and 4, he moves to No. 53.

4   Other hazards are as follows. If a player arrives on No. 6 (The Bridge), he must pay a fee (1 token) and advance to 12. If he arrives on 19 (The Hotellerie), he must pay 1 token and rest there, missing 2 turns. If he arrives on 31, where there is a Well, he must pay 1 token and wait until another player arrives on 31 and extricates him; the second player must then wait his turn at 31. If he arrives on 42 (The Labyrinth), he must pay 1 token and go back to No. 30. If he arrives on 52 (The Prison), he must wait until another player arrives, as for the Well, and takes his place. If he arrives on 58 (Death, denoted by Heads on the ends of Pikes), he must pay 1 token and return to the Start. If, finally, a player is caught up by another arriving on his place, he must pay 1 token and move to his opponent's old number.

5   The winner is the player who first reaches No. 63 (The Palladium of Liberty). He must arrive by the exact score required. If he scores too many, he must double his score and move backwards.

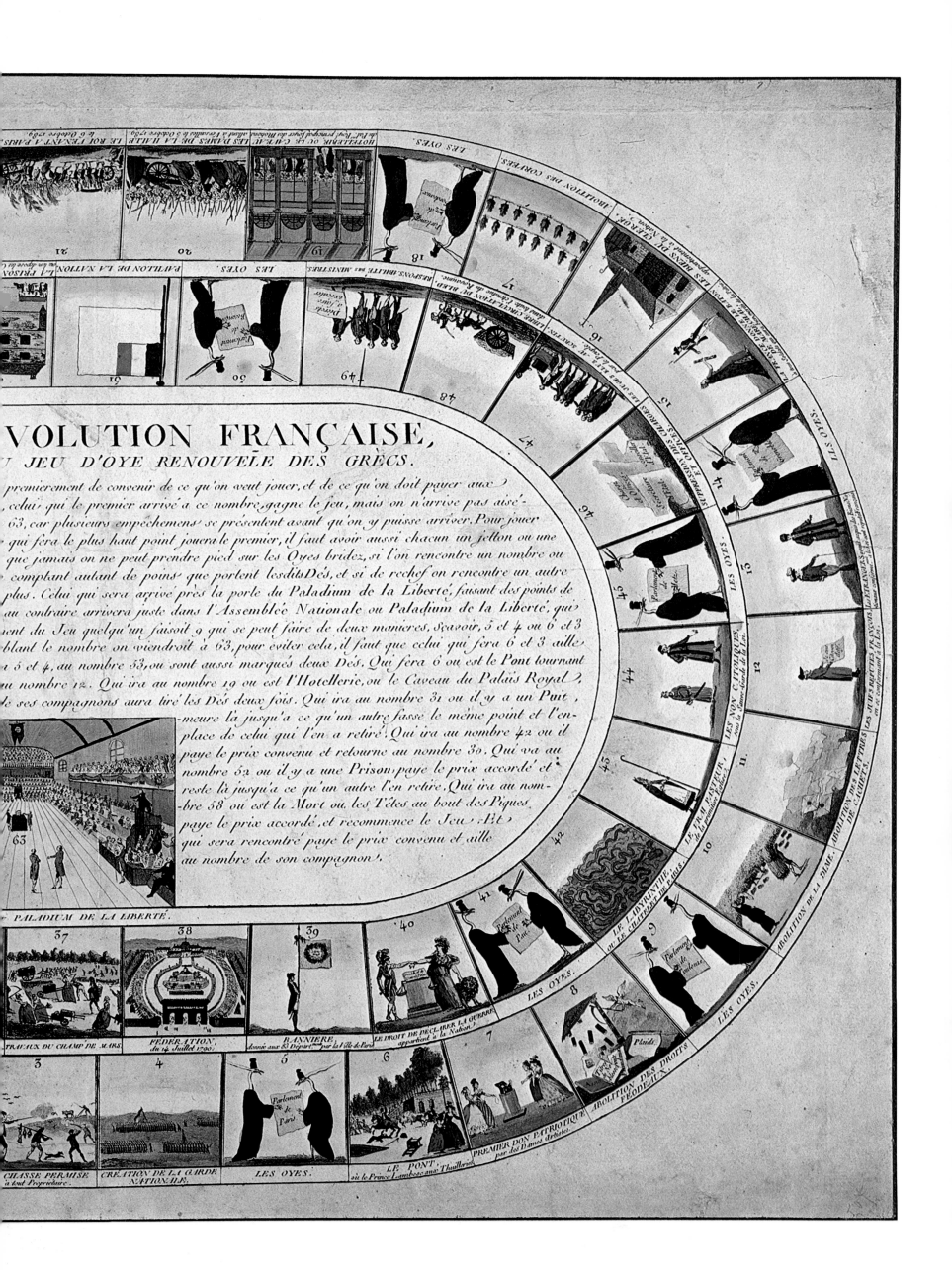

COMIC GAME OF THE GREAT EXHIBITION OF 1851

This amusing boardgame was published in London by William Spooner of 379 Strand. It is based on a satirical booklet that appeared in 1851 under the title of <u>Mr Goggleyes Visit to the Exhibition</u>, and was reputedly written by one Timy Takemin.

The drawings for the 'Comic Game' are attributed to the famous caricaturist George Cruikshank. The Great Exhibition, which was attended by more than 6 million visitors, sparked a large number of commercial ventures that promoted and commemorated it. Among these was another William Spooner game, the 'Illustrative Game of the Great Exhibition', which offered a modest instructional tour of some of the 13,000 exhibits.

1 This is a game for 2–6 players. Each player is given a counter of a different colour, and 4 tokens which he pays into the pool as required. The card with the names of Nations is cut up into 22 separate Prize Tickets, which are placed in the pool.

2 The order of play is determined by throwing the die. The highest scorer begins, the second highest goes next, and so on. The players throw the die and advance by the number indicated. Subsequent moves are made by adding the number scored to the number occupied by the player's counter. Any player making a wrong move through incorrect addition must pay a fine of 3 counters to the pool and return to his former place. If a player arrives at a number already occupied, he must go back to his former place.

3 When a player arrives at a number marked 'Prize', he draws from the pool the Ticket bearing that same number and also the name of a Nation.

4 The game is ended when a player arrives at No. 76, the External View of the Crystal Palace of the Exhibition. The exact number required to reach the 76 mark must be cast. Players who overshoot 76 are to pay a fine of 3 counters to the pool, and return their counter to No. 50. The first player to reach 76 is entitled to the ticket marked 'Game'. All players then exhibit their Prize Tickets.

5 The winner is the player with the greatest number of Prize Tickets. The ticket marked 'Game' is worth 3 Prize Tickets. The winner then takes the pool. If 2 or more players have the same number of Prize Tickets, the pool is divided equally among them, unless the holder of the Game Ticket is in this leading party, in which case he is the winner and takes the pool.

THE SIEGE OF PARIS

Little is known of the origins of this intriguing boardgame. Presumably published after the siege of 1870–71, it proposes a chess-like game around a central island.

1 This is a game for 2, 3 or 5 players. One player commands the Garrison or Fort, the others command elements of the Besieging Party.

2 The Garrison is occupied by 8 Red soldiers – 1 General (G), 1 Colonel (C), and 6 Men (M). Their placing in the Garrison is optional.

3 The Besiegers are 36 strong – 2 Generals (G), 2 Colonels (C), 4 Captains (Ca), 4 Lieutenants (L), and 24 Men (M). These are divided equally into Yellow and Blue counters; Yellow counters move on Black squares only, and Blue counters move on White squares only. At the beginning of the game, the Besiegers are drawn up along the outside lines of the board. The Generals are on the right, the Colonels on the left. Next on each side are 2 Captains. The 4 Lieutenants occupy the centre of the line, and the Men are equally divided in the spaces between the Lieutenants and the Captains.

4 As the aggressors, the Besiegers make the first move, and then each side makes 1 move in turn. Besiegers cannot move backwards, and must also observe the following rules. Generals may move 1, 2 or 3 squares at a time, either forwards, sideways or diagonally. Colonels may move 1 or 2 squares at a time, either forwards or sideways. Captains may move 1 square, forwards or sideways. Lieutenants move diagonally, 1 or 2 squares. Men move diagonally, 1 square. No soldier may change direction in the course of a move, nor jump over any other soldier.

5 The aim of the Besiegers is to capture the Garrison by placing 1 Officer and 3 Men inside it. Once inside, a Besieger cannot be removed.

6 The soldiers of the Garrison aim to beat off the Besiegers and win the game by taking 24 Men and 6 Officers. Garrison soldiers must observe the following rules of movement. The General may move 1 or 2 squares at a time in any direction, on Black or White squares. The Colonel may move 1 or 2 squares at a time, either forwards, backwards or sideways, on Black or White squares. The Men may only move diagonally, forwards or backwards; 3 Men are limited to Black squares, and 3 to White squares.

7 Garrison soldiers 'take' opponents by moving onto and occupying their squares. When a Besieger is taken, he must be unsupported, i.e. there must be no adjacent Besieger capable of occupying his space in 1 move. Once taken, Besiegers are removed from the board. Garrison soldiers are not compelled to take an opponent simply by virtue of their position.

8 Garrison soldiers cannot themselves be taken, but Garrison Men can be blocked in and thereby immobilized. They must then stay in that position until an Officer rescues them.

9 The winner is the side which first achieves its aim (see paragraphs 5 and 6).

RUSSIA VERSUS TURKEY

This British-made battle game was designed and published by James Reeves & Company. The gameboard is illustrated with a Turkish port on the left-hand side and a Russian on the right. The players race in a double spiral across the board and try to take possession of each other's home port. The game was inspired by the fighting between the Turks and the Russians that took place in the early stages of the Crimean War (1853–56). On 4 October 1853 Turkey declared war on Russia. On 30 November the Russian Black Sea Fleet destroyed a Turkish naval squadron off Sinope. This Russian naval victory caused great indignation in Great Britain, and in March 1854 Britain and France both sent fleets into the Black Sea. The following September the Allies began their prolonged siege of the great Russian naval base at Sebastopol.

1   This game may be played by any even number of players. If there are more than 2 players, they should be divided equally into Russians and Turks, and be seated round a table, 1 Russian and 1 Turk alternately.

2   Each player is provided with an appropriately coloured marker, which he places in his home Port before hostilities commence, and tokens with which to pay fines, pilotage, etc. At the beginning, each player pays 2 tokens into the pool.

3   The Russians, as aggressors, begin. One of their number throws the die and moves his counter forward by the number of spaces indicated. The Turk next to him then makes a similar move, leaving his Port towards the Russians, and so on in rotation. Note that Russian moves are numbered in italic type 1–55, and Turkish moves in bold roman type 1–55.

4   As the opposing fleets travel in their spiral voyages across the board, they must observe the various instructions contained in particular spaces. If a Russian or a Turk arrives on a space occupied by an opponent, he is repelled by a broadside and must return to his previous space until his next turn. Any number of ships of the same side may occupy the same space.

5   The Victory is obtained by a majority of whichever side taking possession of the enemy's Port. The victors are entitled to divide the pool as prize money.

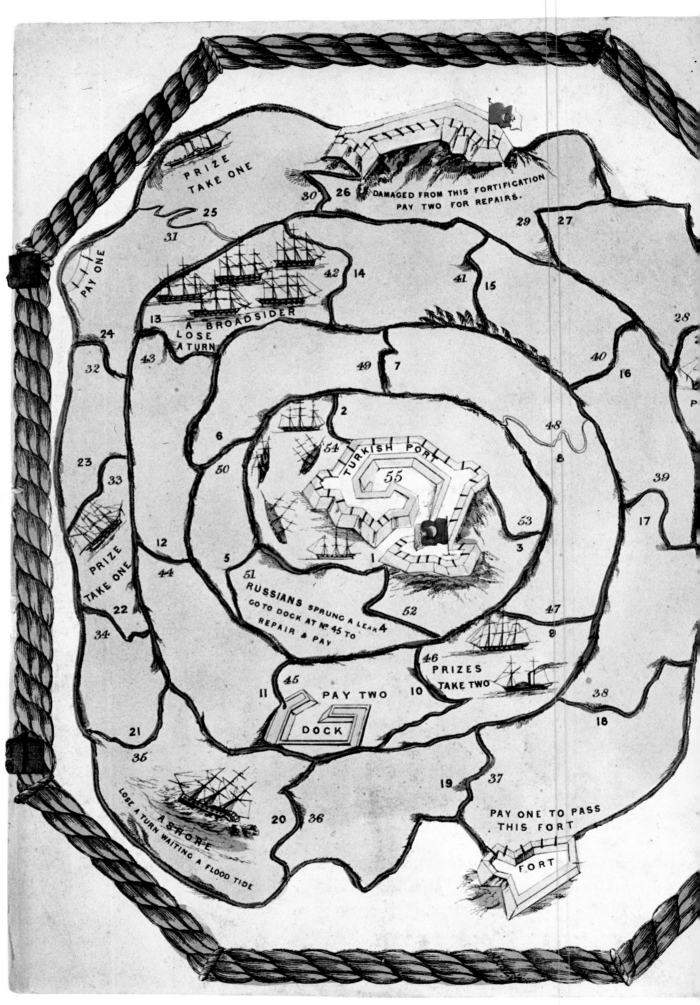

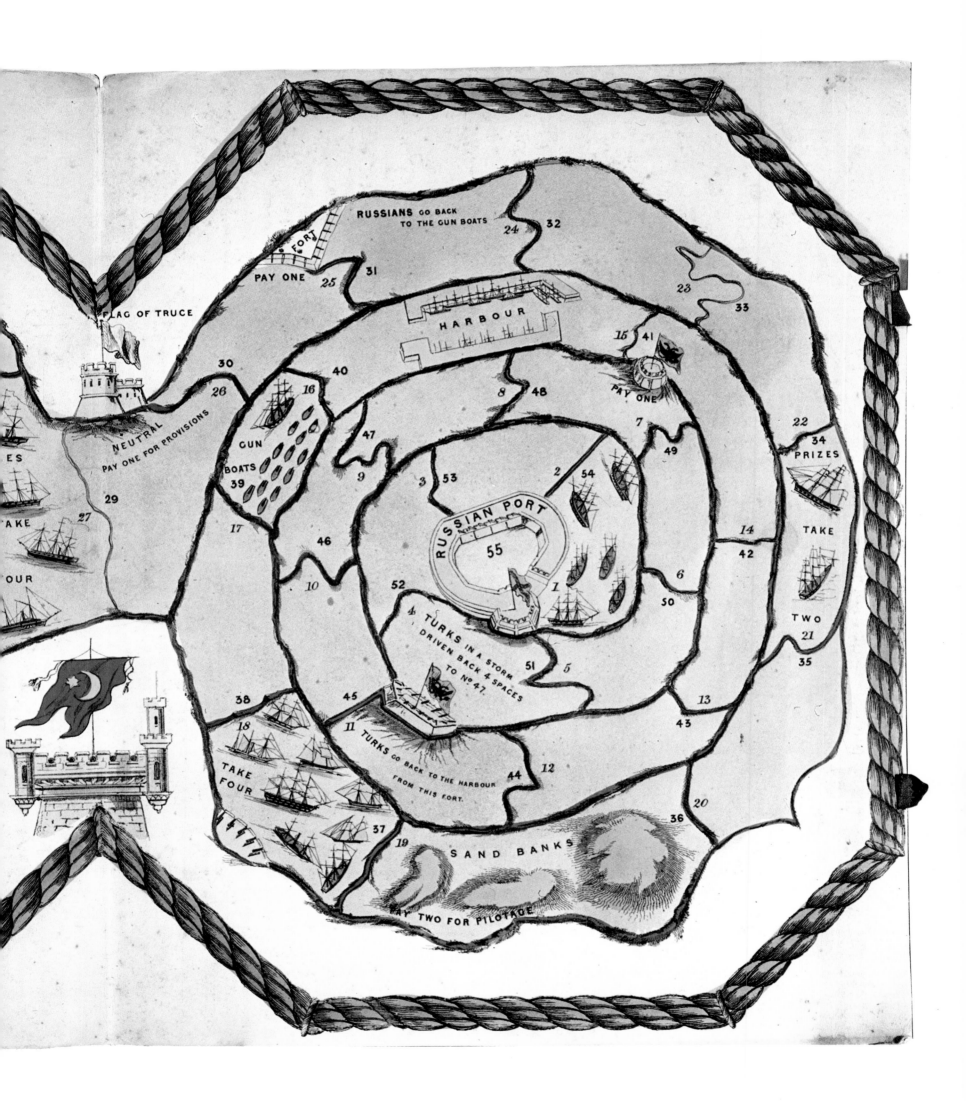

SPYROL

This is probably a variation of the game 'Willy's Walk to See Grandma' that was published in 1869 by A.N. Myers & Co. of Barnes Street, London. The latter game consists of a spiral design printed on a sheet measuring 23 in × 20 in (57 cm × 50 cm), and includes a teetotum and 8 counters of glazed earthenware marked A–H. An example can be seen in the Bethnal Green Museum, London. The 'Spyrol' game illustrated here was issued by the Chad Valley company in 1905.

1 This is a game for 2, 3 or 4 players. Each takes 4 counters of the same colour and places them in the appropriate Corner Enclosures.

2 Players throw the die in turn until a 6 is cast. That player then moves 1 counter into the Start square and throws again, advancing his or her counter by the number indicated. Each time a 6 is thrown, players may bring a new counter onto the board in this way, or may move a counter already in play.

3 Throwing a 6 also entitles a player to a double turn whether or not he is bringing a new counter into play. If he wishes, he may move a different counter after the second throw.

4 Players must advance by the full amount of their throw, whether to their advantage or not. Counters may overtake one another, unless a Barrier has been formed (see below).

5 When a counter is played into a space already occupied by an opponent, it takes the opposing counter's place. The latter is returned to its Corner Enclosure, and must be started again.

6 When 2 or more counters of the same colour are played into the same space, they are placed one upon the other and form a Barrier, which no other piece may seize or pass over.

7 When a counter is played into a space at the foot of a Ladder marked by the feathers of the arrow, it may then be carried to the top of the Ladder provided no other counters occupy any other parts of the Ladder (see Rules 8 and 9).

8 When a counter arrives at any point on a Ladder and an opponent's counter occupies some other space on the Ladder, either above or below it, the new arrival seizes the other, which must be returned to its Corner Enclosure.

9 When some part of the Ladder is occupied by a counter of the same colour, the new arrival must be placed on top of the other to form a Barrier.

10 If an opponent's piece arrives on a Ladder some part of which is occupied by a Barrier, the opponent may not seize the Barrier but, in his turn, the player with the Barrier may jump off the upper counter and seize the opponent. If desired, he may later play the seizing piece back to form the Barrier again, but this move must be in a later turn. In the meantime, an opponent may arrive and seize 1 of the pieces in his turn.

11 To reach Home, the exact number must be thrown, i.e. the mark may not be overshot.

12 If a player cannot move any of his counters in accordance with the rules, he misses that turn.

13 The winner is the player who first gets all 4 counters Home. A counter, once Home, cannot be moved out again.

TWIDDLEUMS

The game of 'Twiddleums' was offered in 4 qualities in the Chad Valley catalogue of 1905, where it was described as 'a very simple game, the rules of which can be mastered in a few minutes but in which considerable opportunities for skill are afforded'.

The board offers a race for up to 6 players, each starting in his or her own enclosure and finishing in another enclosure on the far side of the board. Perhaps it was the game's lack of complication that led the publishers to devise a 'much more exciting' version. (Rules for both are given below.)

1 This is a game for 2–6 players. Each takes a coloured counter and places it in the appropriate Starting Circle. If only 2 players are playing, each may take up to 3 counters; if there are 3 players, each may take 2 counters.

2 Each player in turn moves his or her counter in any direction into an adjoining circle which bears a number consecutive to the occupied circle. Thus a counter in a No. 3 circle may be moved into either a 2 or a 4, but not into a 1, 5 or 6. A counter may not be moved into a circle occupied by an opponent. If a player cannot make an alternative move, he loses that turn.

3 The winner is the first to get his counter or counters into the appropriate Finishing Circle(s).

VARIANT

1 A more exciting version may be played in which counters may be moved in turn either into consecutively numbered circles, as before, or into any adjoining circle occupied by an opponent. When this happens, the opponent's piece is 'taken'.

2 A piece so taken may either be returned to its Starting Circle or removed altogether from the board. Players should agree which version to operate before beginning the game.

3 A player may not miss a turn, whether to his advantage or not, but need not 'take' an opponent unless he wishes to do so.

ROAREM CASTLE

Subtitled 'A New Game of Forfeits', this mild satire of aristocratic life, centred round the Lord of Roarem Castle and his retinue of 3 idle squires and 16 heavily underpaid servants (or so they claim), was published in 1860 by Standring & Company of London.

The game is a race from Nos. 1–32. Each player is equipped with 2 money bags in addition to the usual counter, and is encouraged to engage 2 of the Castle servants by placing a money bag on their respective numbers. The servants' version of their plight is conveyed in a mocking rhyme that accompanied the original rules. This declares:

'We all live by what you give,
Observe our motto plainly;
And can't afford to Roarem's lord,
To let one enter vainly.
For each must pay as well he may,
His presence who would enter;
For who sees him first to favour's thrust,
So play this game and venture,'

50

1 This is a game for 2–4 players. They are known variously as Ploddy, Cloddy, Freddy and Teddy. Each is equipped with a counter of a different colour, which he places at the Start, 2 money bags and a stock of tokens. Before play begins, each places 2 tokens in the pool.

2 The order of play is determined by throwing the die. Whoever throws the highest score begins, the second highest goes next, and so on.

3 The players throw the die in turn and advance by adding the amount indicated to their present score. (The Start position is 1, and a player throwing a 3 would advance initially to 4, and so on).

4 In addition to the fines and rewards marked on the gameboard, there are a number of other hazards, as follows. If a player encounters 1 of the Squires (4, 20, 29), he must miss a turn while paying his respects. If he encounters the Poor Lady (25), he must promise to buy her a new pair of gloves, in consideration of which he moves to 30 and there pays 1 token for his intrusion.

5 Each player has the right to place his 2 money bags on any 2 servants in the game, provided they have not been previously engaged. Any other player arriving on these faithful creatures' numbers must pay 1 token to the pool. The servants are: Porter, Scullery Maid, Black Gardener, Footman, Lady's Maid, Seneschal, Trumpeter, Gamekeeper, Dressmaker, Cook, Coachman, Butler, Waiter.

6 The winner is the player who first reaches 32 (The Lord). The exact number required to finish must be thrown, i.e. the 32 mark may not be overshot. The winner is entitled to the contents of the pool.

THE COTTAGE OF CONTENT
OR RIGHT ROADS AND WRONG WAYS

Published in 1848 by William Spooner, of 379 Strand, London, this game belongs to a genre of 'cross-roads' games, in which the contestants move across the board from junction to junction, their paths determined by whether the totum sends them forwards or backwards, right or left. The firm of William Spooner was producing games in this style at least as early as 1836. Dating from about that time is 'The Journey', or Cross Roads to Conqueror's Castle'. Humorous figures stand about on the roads, some of which bear the same names as roads leading towards the Cottage of Content, e.g. Lackaday Lane and Tittle Tattle Corner.

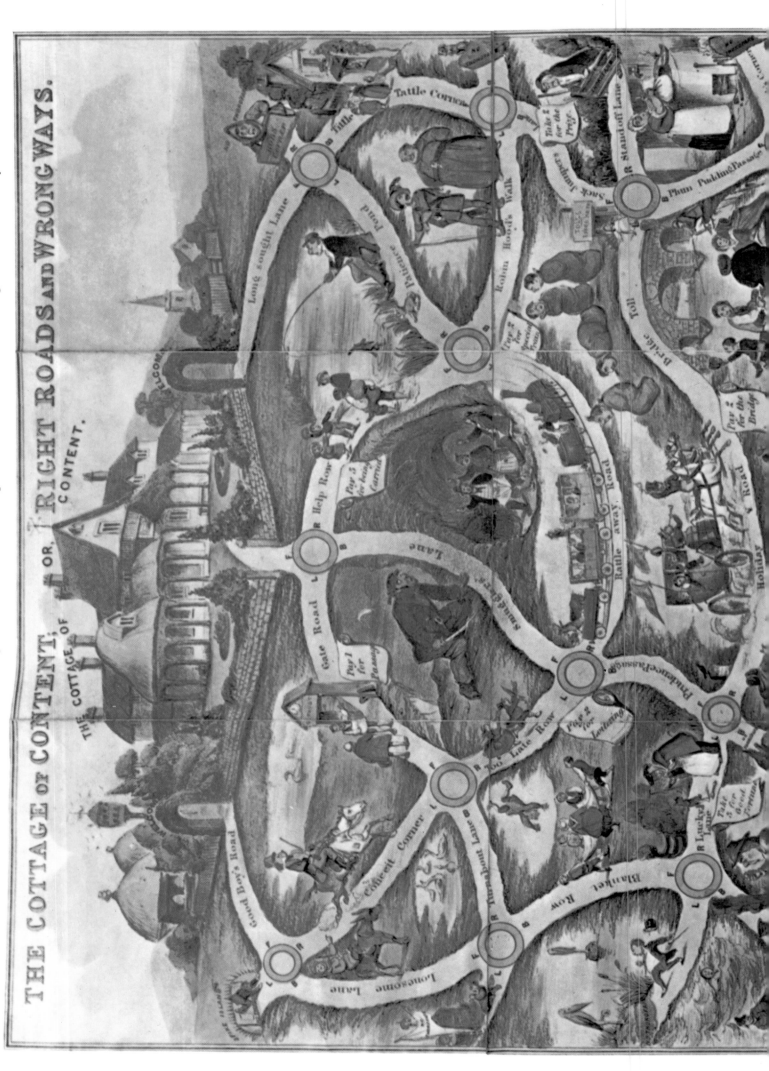

52

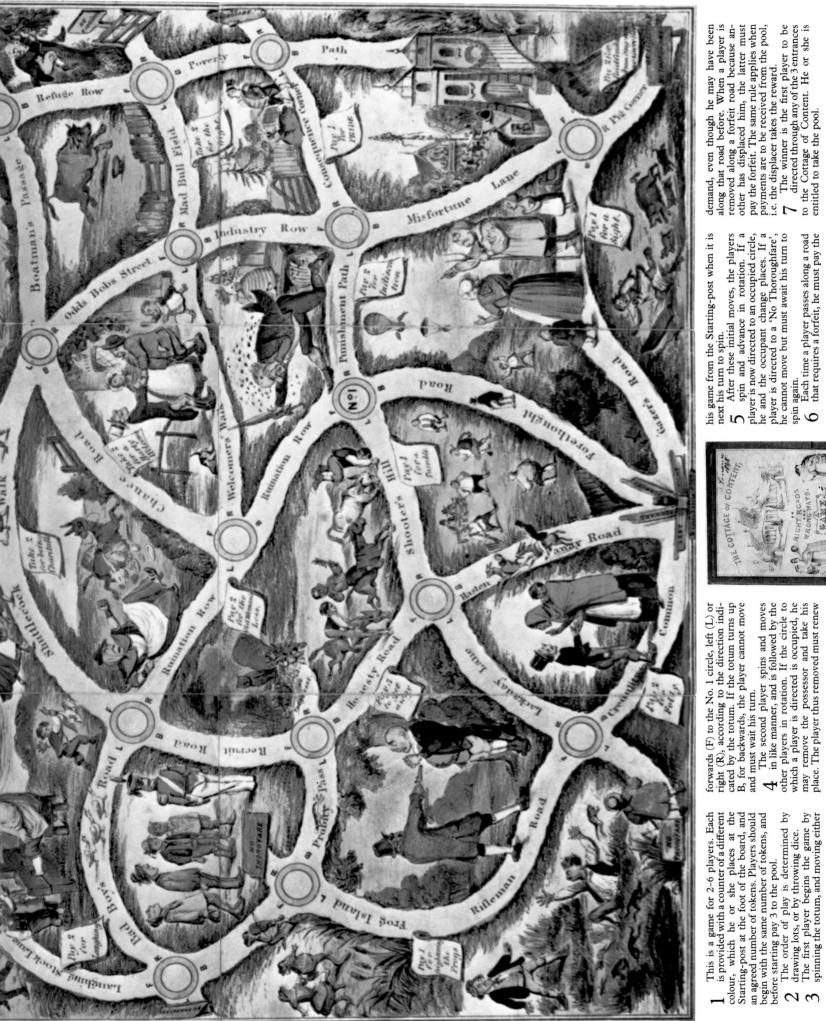

1 This is a game for 2–6 players. Each is provided with a counter of a different colour, which he or she places at the Starting-post at the foot of the board, and begin with the same number of tokens, and before starting pay 3 to the pool.

2 The order of play is determined by drawing lots, or by throwing dice.

3 The first player begins the game by spinning the totum, and moving either forwards (F) to the No. 1 circle, left (L) or right (R), according to the direction indicated by the totum. If the totum turns up B, for backwards, the player cannot move and must wait his turn.

4 The second player spins and moves in like manner, and is followed by the other players in rotation. If the circle to which a player is directed is occupied, he may remove the possessor and take his place. The player thus removed must renew

his game from the Starting-post when it is next his turn to spin.

5 After these initial moves, the players spin and advance in rotation. If a player is now directed to an occupied circle, he and the occupant change places. If a player is directed to a 'No Thoroughfare', he cannot move but must await his turn to spin again.

6 Each time a player passes along a road that requires a forfeit, he must pay the

demand, even though he may have been along that road before. When a player is removed along a forfeit road because another has displaced him, the latter must pay the forfeit. The same rule applies when payments are to be received from the pool, i.e. the displacer takes the reward.

7 The winner is the first player to be directed through any of the 3 entrances to the Cottage of Content. He or she is entitled to take the pool.

AN ECCENTRIC EXCURSION TO THE CHINESE EMPIRE

In 1843 William Spooner brought out this bizarre and highly entertaining 'cross-roads' game. As the accompanying rule book explains:
'The ECCENTRIC EXCURSION TO CHINA is to be performed by four

different modes of travelling:
1. By STEAM-BOAT.
2. By WALKING.
3. By the AERIAL, or FLYING MACHINE.
4. By RAILWAY.'

Each traveller moves at first according to his code letter (S, W, A, or R) or 1 other which is deemed compatible (see detailed rules below). From the second round onwards, however, chaos breaks out as the travellers abandon their alloted modes and

virtually give themselves up to fate. For the rest of the game they trek across a weird landscape of bogs, streams and fields, peopled by strange natives. The winner is the first to arrive at a 'Game' circle at the top of the board.

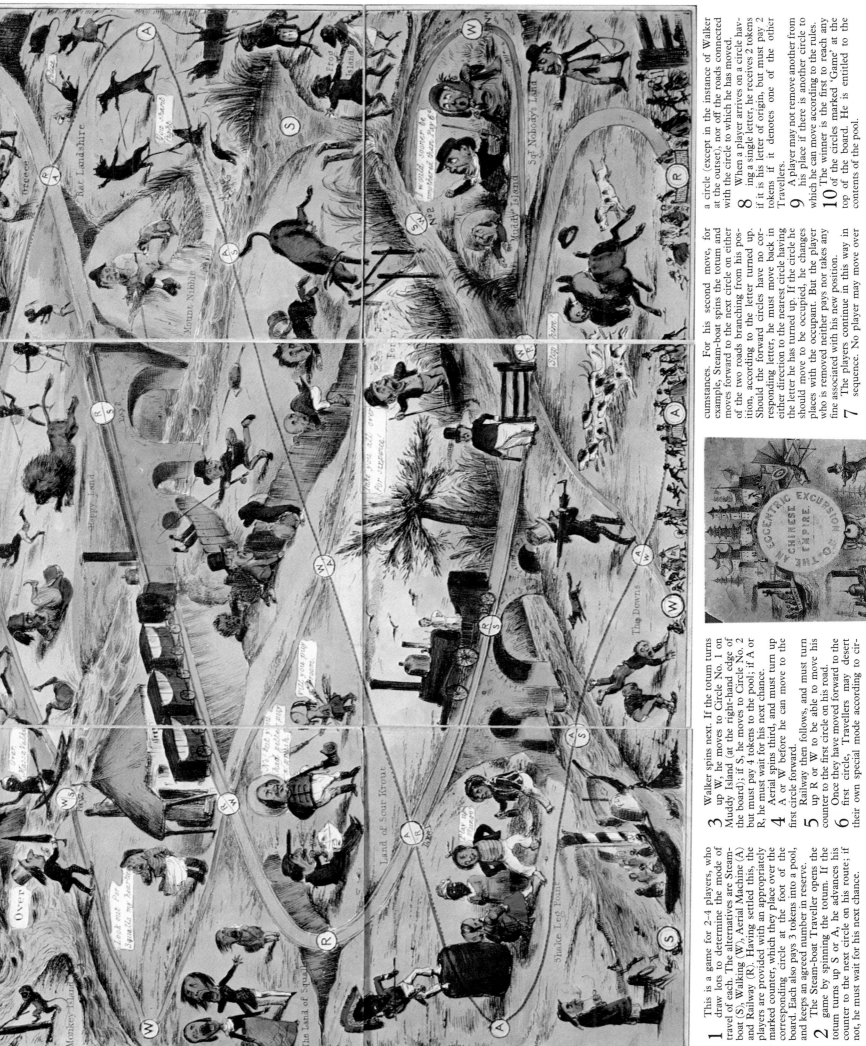

1 This is a game for 2–4 players, who draw lots to determine the mode of travel of each. The alternatives are Steam-boat (S), Walking (W), Aerial Machine (A) and Railway (R). Having settled this, the players are provided with an appropriately marked counter, which they place over the corresponding circle at the foot of the board. Each also pays 3 tokens into a pool, and keeps an agreed number in reserve.

2 The Steam-boat Traveller opens the game by spinning the totum. If the totum turns up S or A, he advances his counter to the next circle on his route; if not, he must wait for his next chance.

3 Walker spins next. If the totum turns up W, he moves to Circle No. 1 on Muddy Island (at the right-hand edge of the board); if S, he moves to Circle No. 2 but must pay 4 tokens to the pool; if A or R, he must wait for his next chance.

4 Aerial spins third, and must turn up A or W before he can move to the first circle forward.

5 Railway then follows, and must turn up R or W to be able to move his counter to the first circle on his road.

6 Once they have moved forward to the first circle, Travellers may desert their own special mode according to cir-

cumstances. For his second move, for example, Steam-boat spins the totum and moves forward to the next circle on either of the two roads branching from his position, according to the letter turned up. Should the forward circles have no corresponding letter, he must move back in either direction to the nearest circle having the letter he has turned up. If the circle he should move to be occupied, he changes places with the occupant. But the player who is removed neither pays nor takes any fine associated with his new position.

7 The players continue in this way in sequence. No player may move over a circle (except in the instance of Walker at the outset), nor off the roads connected with the circle to which he has moved.

8 When a player arrives on a circle having a single letter, he receives 2 tokens if it is his letter of origin, but must pay 2 tokens if it denotes one of the other Travellers.

9 A player may not remove another from his place if there is another circle to which he can move according to the rules.

10 The winner is the first to reach any of the circles marked 'Game' at the top of the board. He is entitled to the contents of the pool.

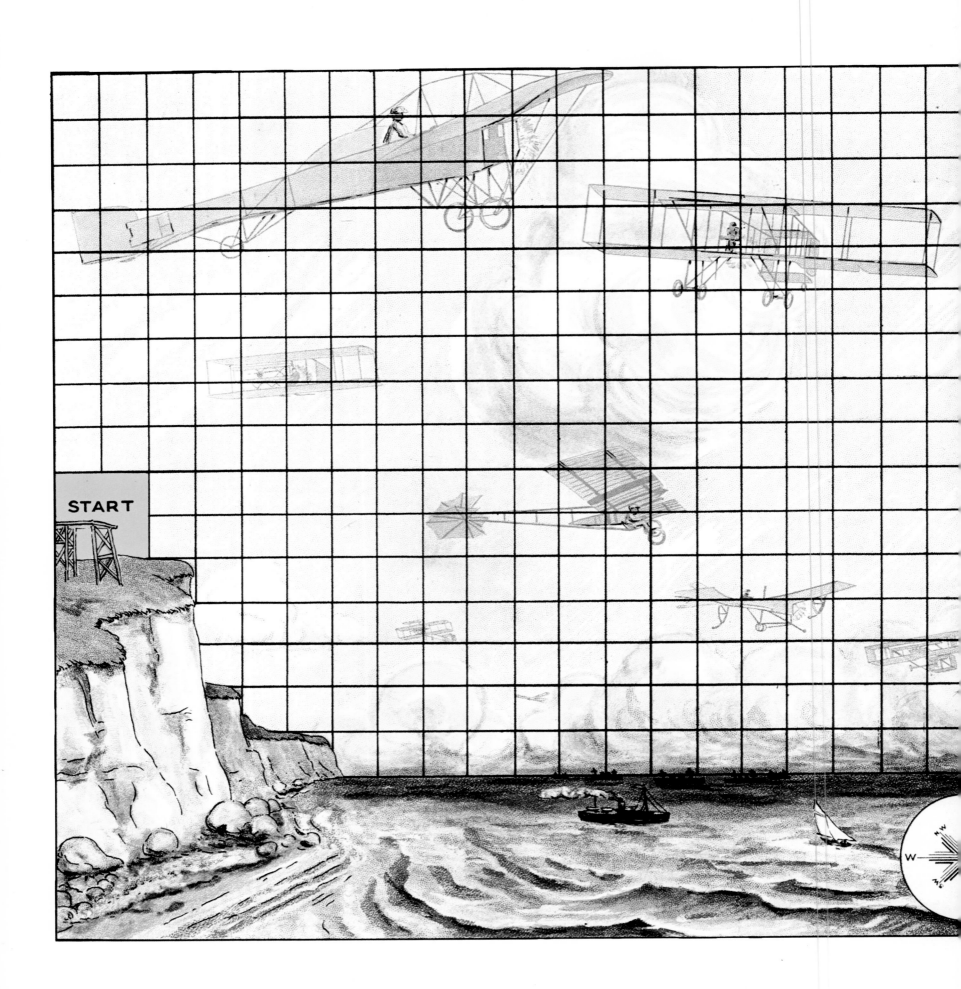

START

AERO FLIGHTS

'Aero Flights' was published by Chad Valley in 1910. By then, William Spooner's intimations of travel by 'the aerial, or flying machine' (see previous pages) were much more than fantasy. This game was no doubt inspired by the first successful cross-Channel flight, made on 25 July 1909 by Louis Blériot from Les Boraques, near Calais, to Dover. His 37-minute crossing won him a <u>Daily Mail</u> prize of £1,000. The object of the game is to emulate Blériot, but in the reverse direction. Starting from the English coast, the players or Fliers guide their aircraft eastwards to France.

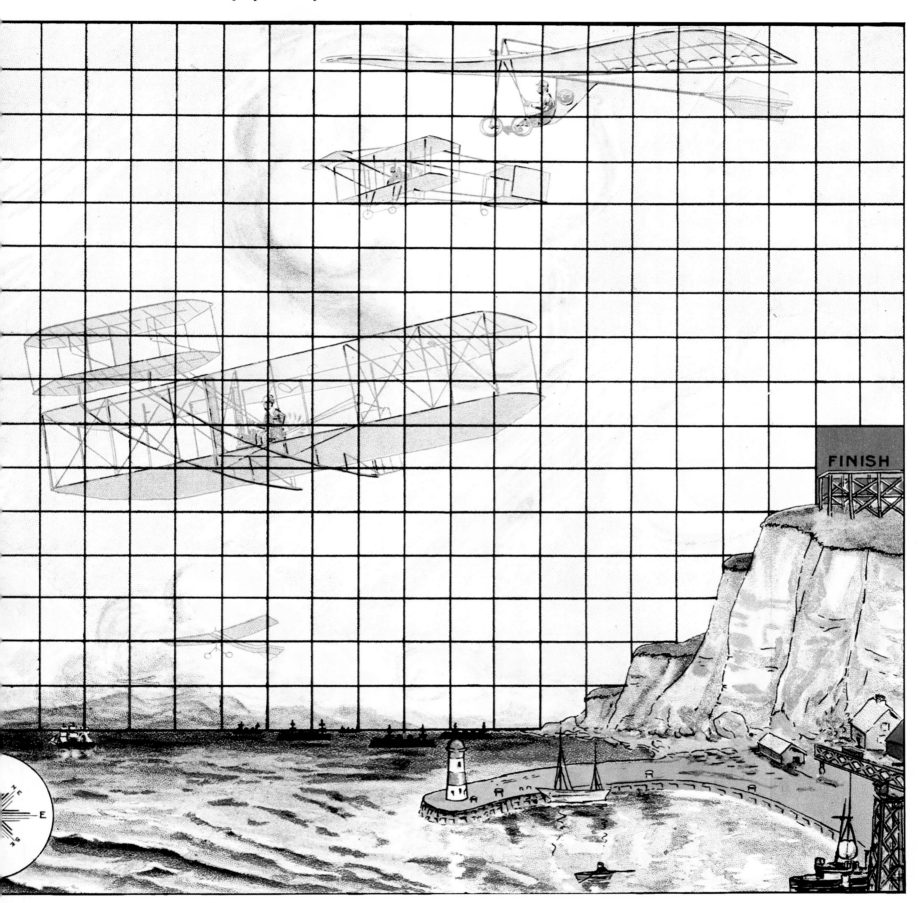

1 This is a game for 2–6 players, or Fliers. Each takes a counter of a different colour and places it by the Start ramp.

2 The order of play is determined by throwing the die. The highest scorer begins, the second highest goes next, and so on. The object is to beat the other Fliers across the Channel and land on the opposite clifftop.

3 The Fliers throw the die in turn, and may move in a straight line in any direction they choose by the amount indicated. This applies except when a 5 or 6 is thrown; they must then spin the 8-sided

Compass Spinner to determine in which direction they must move. Fliers must advance by the full amount of their throw. If at the start of the race they find it impossible to move, e.g. the Compass sends them West, they miss that turn.

4 Similarly, Fliers whose throw would take them beyond the edges of the sky, at the top or sides of the board, miss that turn.

5 Fliers dropping into the sea are rescued by patrol boat and may return to the Start. Fliers falling onto the Cliffs on either side of the Channel suffer irreparable damage and are withdrawn from the race.

6 Aerial collisions. If a Flier arrives on a square occupied by another Flier, both throw the die to determine the outcome of their collision. The player with the higher score carries on by that number in a direction determined by the Compass. The player with the lower score must drop South by the number thrown. If this takes him into the sea, he must return to the Start, as usual.

7 The winner is the player who first lands his aircraft on one of the squares at the Finish. The exact number is not essential, i.e. overshooting is tolerated on the winning throw.

THE DIVER'S LUCK

In this simple race for undersea treasure, modestly described by Chad Valley, the publishers, as the 'most smartly produced game ever put upon the market', 2 Divers descend by rope to the ocean floor. Exotic fish flood past them as they weave a circuitous course towards the Gold at No. 100.

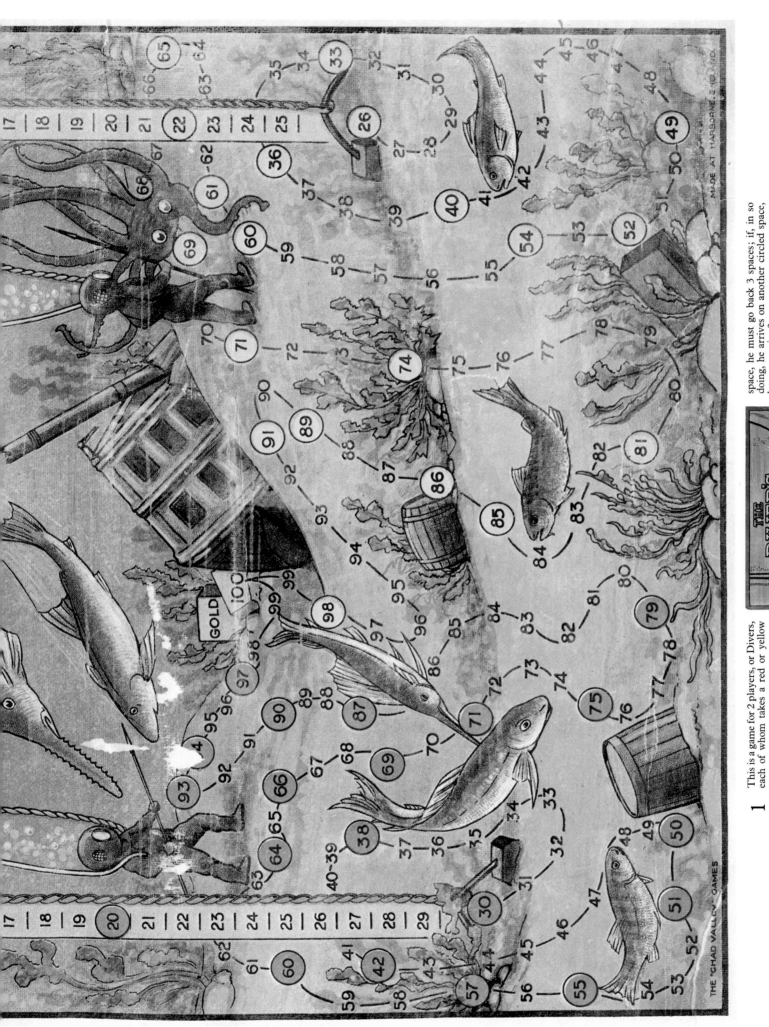

1   This is a game for 2 players, or Divers, each of whom takes a red or yellow counter.

2   The order of play is determined by throwing the die. The higher scorer begins.

3   The Divers throw the die in turn and advance down the rope by the score indicated. If a Diver arrives on a circled space, he must go back 3 spaces; if, in so doing, he arrives on another circled space, he must retire 3 more spaces.

4   The winner is the first player to reach the Gold at No. 100. To finish, the exact number must be thrown, i.e. the 100 mark must not be overshot; players so doing must count up to 100 and go back again by the amount of the excess.

MARATHON RACE

The route in this Chad Valley game of 1910 is modelled on the marathon course followed by competitors in that event in the Olympics of 1908. It runs between Windsor Castle and White City Stadium. The real-life race was made famous by the Dorando Pietri incident. Pietri, a frail Italian, was first into the White City Stadium but, almost completely exhausted, he repeatedly fell and was assisted across the finishing line by two officials. For this, Pietri was disqualified and the event was awarded to Johnny Hayes (USA) who finished in 2 hours 55 minutes 18.4 seconds. Some 250,000 people watched the race, and afterwards Pietri was given a special gold cup by Queen Alexandra.

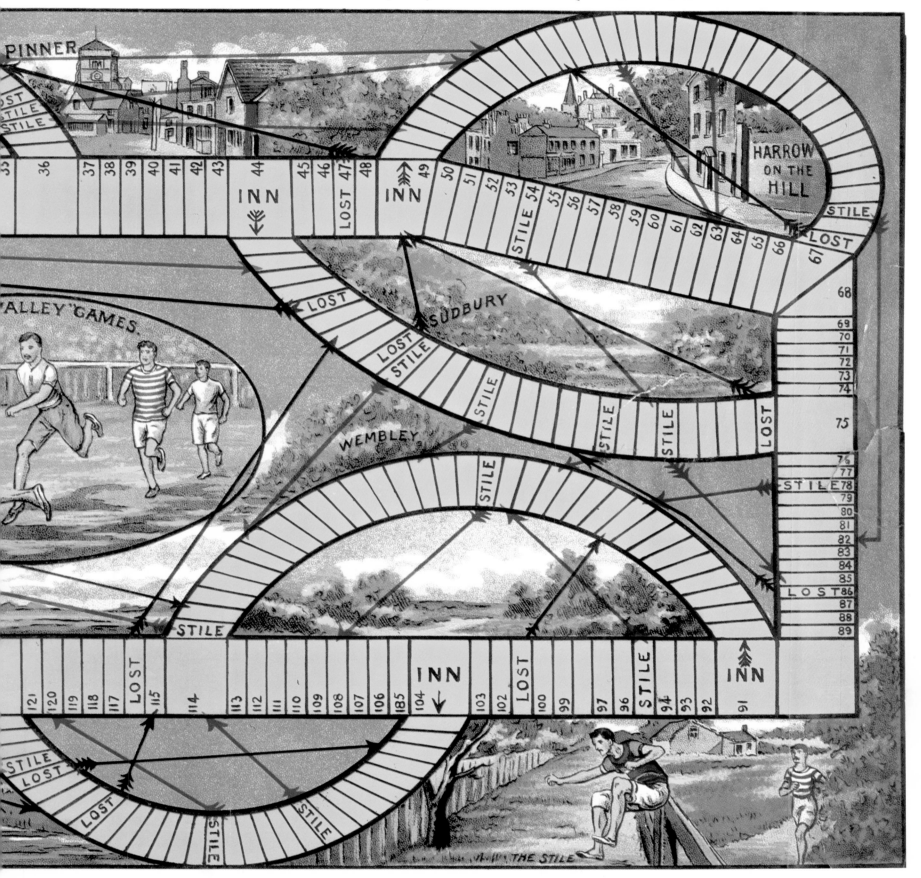

1 This is a game for 2–6 players. Each is provided with a counter of a different colour and places it on the Starting Grid at Windsor.

2 The order of play is determined by throwing the dice. The highest scorer starts, the second highest goes next, etc.

3 Players throw the dice and move in turn by the total scored. If a Runner arrives on a space marked 'Inn', he must take the detour shown. If he arrives at a Stile, he may jump forward as indicated by the arrow. If he is Lost, he must go back to the position at the arrowhead. (At 19 there

is an artist's error; the base of the arrow, i.e. the feathers, should be shown here, not the head). At 150, players should continue in their present direction, either moving through to 151 or crossing to the detour.

4 To finish, Runners must arrive exactly on 167; if they overshoot, they must count up to 167 and then go backwards by the amount of the excess. Once arrived on 167, Runners enter the Stadium and line up behind one another, ready for the presentation of the (imaginary) Trophy.

5 The winner is the first player to reach 167.

TRENCHO

The principle behind this 1917 game is taken from 'Nine Men's Morris', a game that was popular in Europe as much as 500 years ago. 'Blind Man's Morris', 'Marris', 'Merelles', 'Merril', 'Mill', 'Merry Hole', and 'Peg Meryll' are some of the other names by which this game is known. Merel is an Old French word for a coin or counter.

In these early games, as in 'Trencho' (subtitled 'The Famous Australian War Game'), 2 players each with 9 counters attempt to outmanoeuvre each other in alternate moves.

Other games inspired by the fighting on the Western Front were 'In the Trenches', 'Shell Fort', and 'Fall In'.

RULES FOR

"Trencho" is a game for two, and
The object of the game is to cap
in a straight line in one tren
It is, of course, the aim of each pi
The players toss for first, and the
the gun positions, when all th
by moving only along a tren
When three men are in a straight li
nected trench, the player obta
opponents men from the boa
viously forfeited, but it is no
with this man.
The same trench cannot be capt
being necessary to employ on
is won by the player who firs
COPYRIGHT REGISTERED

The rules listed below are an expanded and, we hope, somewhat clearer version of those appearing on the gameboard.

1 This is a game for 2 players, each of whom is provided with 9 counters or Men in different colours.

2 The opponents toss a coin to decide who shall start, then they alternately place their Men on gun positions of their choice. The object is to capture trenches by placing 3 Men in a straight line on 3 gun positions.

3 When all the Men are on the board, play continues by alternately moving 1 Man along a trench by 1 gun position. Men may also be switched from 1 trench to another along the zig-zag saps or connecting trenches.

4 When 3 Men are in a straight line along the same trench, the player may remove 1 of his opponent's Men from the board. Alternatively, he may restore 1 of his own Men previously forfeited. If he chooses the latter course, he may not use the restored Man immediately to complete a line of 3.

5 A trench may not be captured again by the same 3 Men; 1 new Man must enter each 'scoring' line of 3. Lines of 3 along the zig-zag saps do not count.

6 The winner is the player who first reduces his opponent to 2 Men.

BOBBIES & THIEVES

In this ingenious chase game, 3 Bobbies (so named after Sir Robert Peel, the British reformer) pursue 3 Thieves and try to arrest and imprison them by landing on their spaces, after which the felons are committed to jail. Each figure enters play when a 1 is thrown. The Bobbies start from inside the Prison, and the Thieves bolt from the House and head for the cover of the Wood.

If 2 Thieves manage to enter the Wood, the victory is theirs (and crime is seen to pay). Justice is done, on the other hand, if the Bobbies catch and imprison 2 Thieves, provided always that the third Thief is not still at large on the board.

1 This is a game for 2 players. One takes the 3 Bobby counters and the other the 3 Thief counters. The Bobbies start the game at the Prison, and the Thieves in the House.

2 Players throw the die in turn. A 1 is needed to move a Bobby from Prison or a Thief from the House. Once a counter is in play, moves are made in a straight line according to the number indicated. If he chooses, a player may miss a turn.

3 The Thieves aim to pass from the House into the cover of the Wood, and the Bobbies try to catch and imprison the Thieves. They can do this by moving by the exact value of the throw onto a space occupied by a Thief, in which case the latter is removed immediately to Prison. The Bobby then takes his place on the

Board – provided there is at least 1 other Bobby in the Prison to guard the captured Thief. If there is no other Bobby in Prison, the capturing Bobby must go back there to guard his prisoner.

4 A Bobby may play 'over' a Thief, but a Thief may not play 'over' a Bobby. If the Thief can make no other move, he loses his turn.

5 If a Thief is played into a space occupied by a Bobby, at the player's option the Thief either takes his place and the Bobby is returned immediately to Prison, or another Thief may be released from Prison, to be started again from the House in the usual way. In the latter event, the first Thief returns to his original position, since no space may be occupied by more than 1 piece at the same time. An imprisoned Thief may also be released when another Thief safely reaches the Wood. To enter the Wood, a Thief may not overstep the last space; the exact number must be thrown or the turn missed.

6 The winner is the 'Thief' player who gets 2 Thieves into the Wood, or the 'Bobby' player who gets 2 Thieves imprisoned when there is no other left in play.

BAGATELLE

This 1913 game is a tiddleywinks version of the cue-and-ball game usually associated with the name 'Bagatelle'. In place of holes at the far end of the board, this game offers flat circular targets at which the players 'flit' their counters. The mechanical pinball machines found in cafés, bars, and amusement arcades are a development of the 'Bagatelle' game, and several domestic versions have been produced that are also called 'Bagatelle'.

In many of these mechanical games the targets are holes or protected areas entered through a narrow opening or 'gate'; these are usually scattered all over the board (rather than placed at the top only, as in our game).

N.B. Players are advised to use plastic counters (not provided) for this game, since ordinary cardboard counters cannot usually be made to 'flit' far enough.

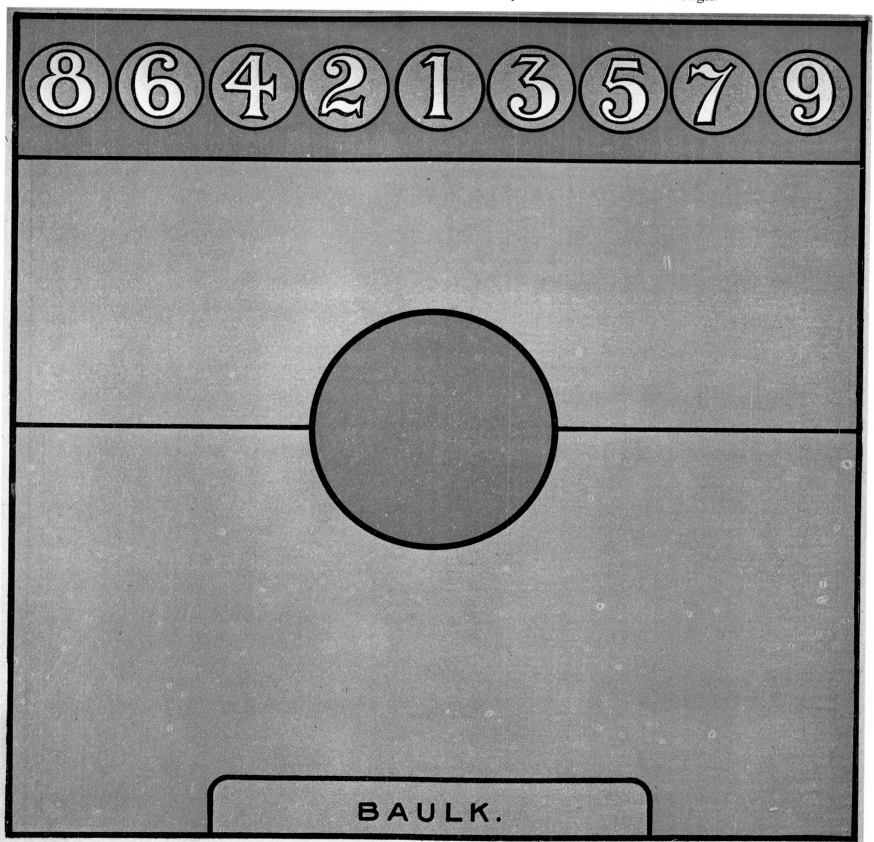

1 This is a game for any number of players. Each in turn plays with all 9 counters, which he places 1 at a time in baulk.

2 By pressing on the edge of the counter, he then jumps or 'flits' it towards the other end.

3 Counters falling on the small circles at the upper end score according to the numbers indicated. If a counter falls upon 2 circles, its score is that of the higher number. A counter scores if it merely touches a circle. If it falls entirely within a circle, its score is doubled.

4 If a counter rests wholly or partly upon another, the upper counter fails

to score. The Red counter scores double every time, whether as a gain or a loss.

5 Counters falling wholly or partly inside the Red central circle may be 'flitted' again from where they rest. Counters which fail to 'flit' into the central circle, or over the transverse black line, or which jump off the board altogether, lose 1 point (as before, the Red counter loses double, i.e. 2 points).

6 A player's score is totalled at the end of his complete turn. The positions of counters may be altered by others falling upon them, but only their final positions count.

7 The winner is the player with the highest number of points after an agreed number of turns.

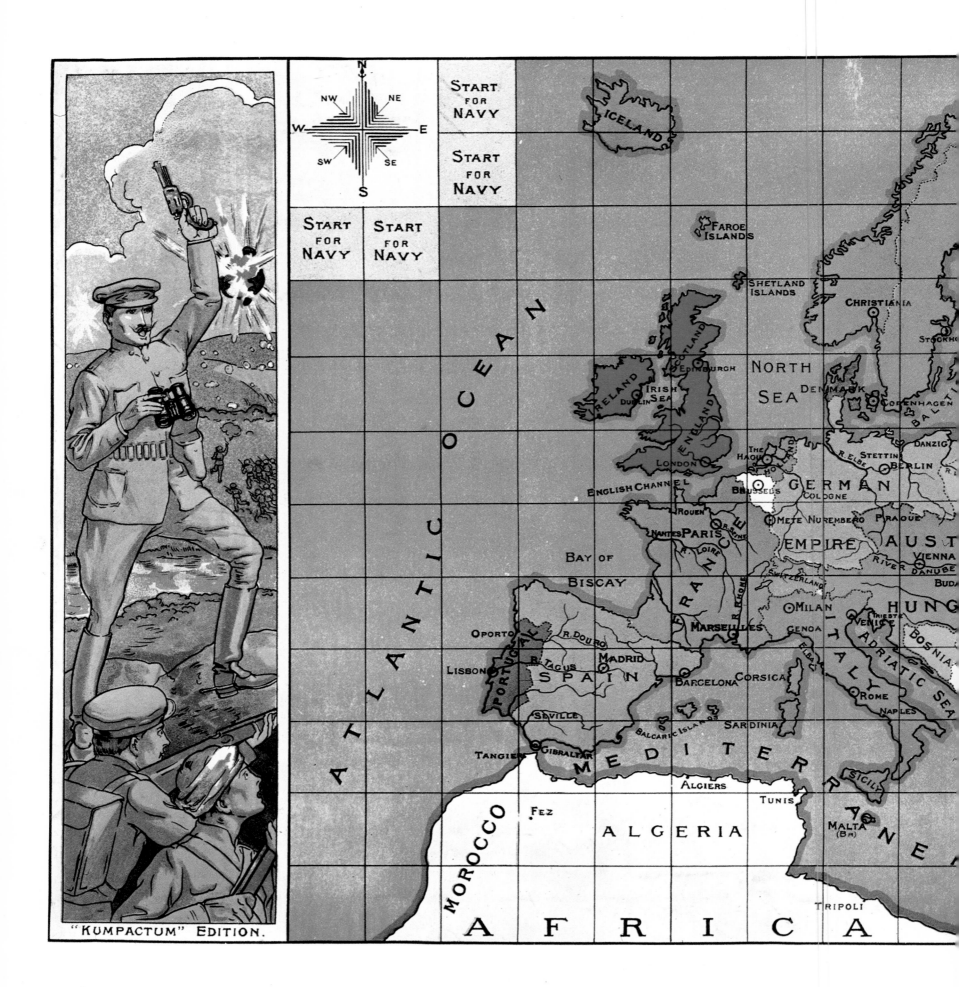

THE INVASION OF EUROPE

One of a number of strategic war games produced in the years leading up to the Great War, this game sets 2 invasion forces against each other – a 4-strong Naval body versus a 5-strong Army. Their common aim in this adapted version of the game is to secure possession of Europe by placing all members of their respective forces on squares containing ringed cities. The disparity in their numbers is offset by the greater choice that the Army Commander can exercise in planning moves. An added complication is provided by the Compass spinner, which dictates the direction of all moves; if either commander is unable to move a single one of his units as directed, he must say 'Pass', and offer the move to his opponent. This game was first published by Chad Valley in 1910.

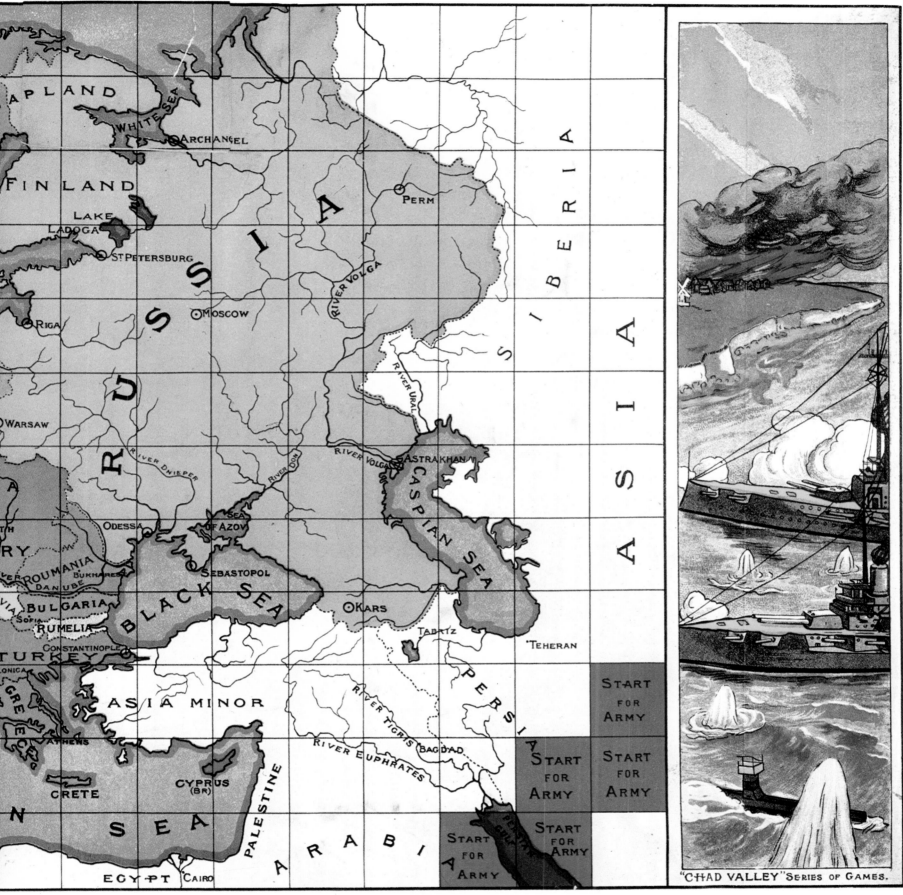

"CHAD VALLEY" SERIES OF GAMES.

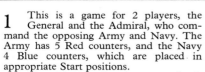

1 This is a game for 2 players, the General and the Admiral, who command the opposing Army and Navy. The Army has 5 Red counters, and the Navy 4 Blue counters, which are placed in appropriate Start positions.

2 The objective of each commander is to place his entire force on squares bearing ringed cities.

3 The General and the Admiral toss a coin to determine who shall start. Each then in turn throws the die and spins the 8-sided Compass, and moves 1 unit in accordance with these movement orders. If one side is unable to move by the full amount indicated, he must say 'Pass', and thereby offer the move to his enemy. The other commander has the option either of using the move offered, or of throwing and spinning again.

4 Naval units may move freely across land, and Army units across water. Units may jump over each other's positions, whether friend or foe, but no 2 units may occupy the same position. If a unit at the end of a move would land on a square occupied by an enemy unit, he may challenge him for possession of it. The outcome is determined by throwing the die: if the challenger throws the higher score, the 2 units change places; if the defender wins, no change occurs and the defending side makes the next throw.

5 The winner is the commander who first completes the Invasion of Europe by getting all his units onto ringed cities.

DAY OF A YOUNG MOUSE
OR LA JOURNÉE D'UN SOURICEAU

Alison Uttley's stories and Margaret Tempest's drawings of Little Grey Rabbit and her friends have delighted children for many years. This diverting and educational game is based on a set of drawings by Margaret Tempest. It tells the story of a mischievous young Mouse's day from the moment he gets up in the morning until he is tucked up in bed again and asleep. Each frame contains a number spelled out in French, and some also include a simple commentary and instructions.

The game takes the form of a race from Nos. 1–100. As each player arrives on a number, he or she reads aloud the French words printed there, and then carries out any special directions. To help beginners in French, a translation is also included.

1 This is a game for 2–6 players. Each is provided with a counter or Mouse of a different colour and places it beside No. 1.

2 The order of play is determined by throwing the die. The highest scorer starts, the second highest goes next, and so on.

3 Players throw the die and move in turn by the number indicated. On arriving at a new space, the player reads aloud the number and any special instructions contained there. He then carries out the instructions.

4 The winner is the first to play his Mouse through the day and see him safely asleep in bed (No. 100). The exact number required to finish must be thrown, i.e. the 100 mark may not be overshot.

SPECIAL INSTRUCTIONS TRANSLATED

1. He is in his bed.
3. He gets up. Go to 5.
6. He gets washed. Go to 7.
8. He has his breakfast. Go to 10.
11. He spills his milk. Go back to 7.
13. He leaves for school. Go to 14.
15. He drops his books. Go back to 12.
18. He arrives late. Go back to 16.
20. He knows his lessons well. Go to 24.
22. He gets the dunce's cap (literally 'He has the donkey's cap'). Go back to 17.
25. On his way home. Go to 26.
28. He fights with a friend. Go back to 23.
30. Lunch is served. Go to 31.
32. It's hot and he burns his tongue. Go back to 27.
35. He explores the Mayor's house. Go back to 33.
37. He arrives in the kitchen. Go to 39.
38. He eats cakes on the sideboard. Go back to 36.
40. The cook arrives. He falls in the flour. Go back to 34.
41. He goes into the dining room. Go to 43.
44. A cigarette is on the mantelshelf. He smokes it. Go back to 36.
47. He feels sick. Go back to 42.
49. He feels better and climbs up the candle. Go to 50.
51. He looks about him. Go to 52.
54. The cat is looking at him. He doesn't dare come down. Go back to 46.
56. He falls in the inkstand. Go back to 48.
58. The cat runs after him. Go back to 50.
60. He escapes from it. Go to 66.
61. His mother is waiting impatiently for him. Go to 62.
63. She scolds him. Go back to 59.
65. She sends him to bed. Go back to 57.
68. He has his bath. Go to 70.
71. He gets soap in his eye. Go back to 67.
73. His mother dries him with a towel. Go to 75.
76. He says good evening to his father. Go to 77.
78. He steals a tart in the larder. Go back to 55.
80. His mother spanks him. Go back to 64.
83. He cleans his teeth (literally 'He washes his teeth'). Go to 85.
86. He hides in a basket. Go back to 69.
87. His mother finds him. Go back to 79.
90. He jumps into his bed. Go to 92.
93. His mother brings him something to eat. Go to 94.
95. He breaks his plate. Go back to 85.
97. His mother tucks him up. Go to 98.
100. He goes to sleep.

SINNET

In 'Sinnet' ('Tennis' backwards), the players shuttle a ball/counter back and forth across the net according to the throw of a die. The ball must always move forwards, and scoring is the same as for Lawn Tennis. Players thus have the option of playing out a full 3 or 5-set match, in championship style, or of settling for a shorter version based on the first to an agreed number of games.

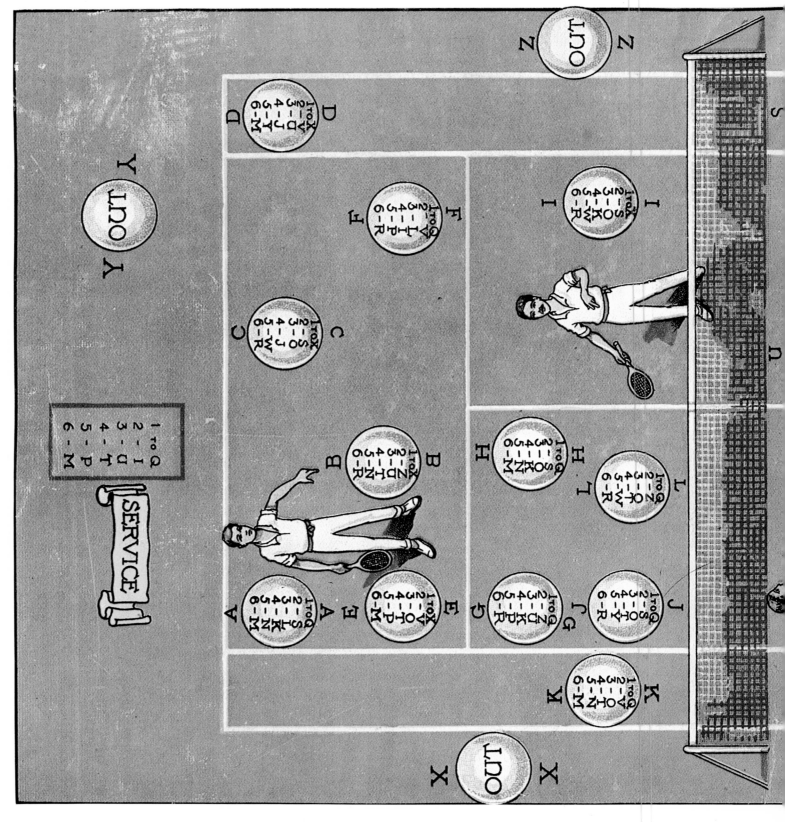

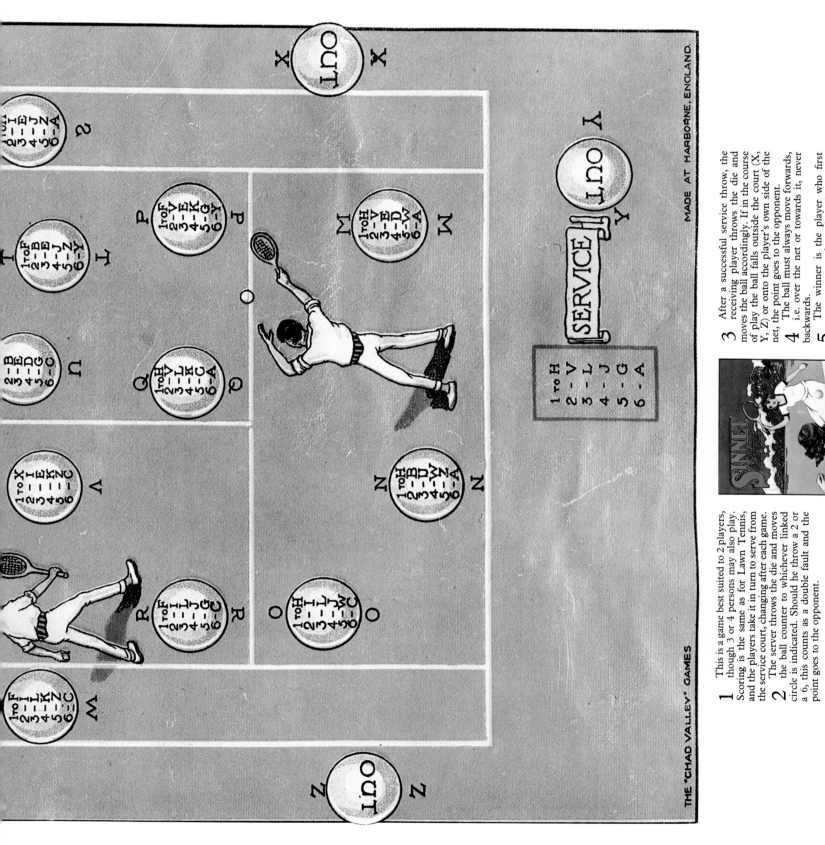

THE "CHAD VALLEY" GAMES

MADE AT HARBORNE, ENGLAND.

1 This is a game best suited to 2 players, though 3 or 4 persons may also play. Scoring is the same as for Lawn Tennis, and the players take it in turn to serve from the service court, changing after each game.

2 The server throws the die and moves the ball counter to whichever linked circle is indicated. Should he throw a 2 or a 6, this counts as a double fault and the point goes to the opponent.

3 After a successful service throw, the receiving player throws the die and moves the ball accordingly. If in the course of play the ball falls outside the court (X, Y, Z) or onto the player's own side of the net, the point goes to the opponent.

4 The ball must always move forwards, i.e. over the net or towards it, never backwards.

5 The winner is the player who first scores an agreed number of games, or sets as in Lawn Tennis.

START

FINISH

THE "CHAD VALLEY" GAMES

STEEPLECHASE

Chad Valley produced several horseracing games in the early decades of this century. These included 'The Hunt Cup' (1910), 'The Grand National Steeplechase' (1910), see label below, 'The Stirrup Cup' (1922), and the present game, which appeared in 1923. The company also made a range of mechanical horse games, of which 'Escalado' (1933) was the most successful. 'Steeplechase' is a straightforward race game from Nos. 1–100. Horses are penalized at certain fences, and have to drop out of the race if they land in the Stream (at Nos. 65 and 82).

MADE AT HARBORNE ENGLAND.

starts, the second highest goes next, and so on.

3 Players throw the die and move in turn by the number indicated. If a player arrives on a simple Fence, he misses a turn. If he arrives on a Horse and Rider space, he may advance 2 further spaces for going well. Exceptions to the latter are Nos. 41 and 61 (Jockey Thrown and Riderless Horse respectively), which mean the Horse must return to the Start. If a player lands in the Stream (Nos. 65 and 82), the Horse is declared fallen and is withdrawn from the race.

1 This is a game for 2 or more players. Each is provided with a counter or Horse of a different colour, and places it on the Start line.

2 The order of play is determined by throwing the die. The highest number

4 The winner is the player whose Horse first arrives at the Finish (No. 100). The exact number required must be thrown, i.e. the Winning Post may not be overshot.

BUSY BEES

Published in 1922 by Chad Valley, who described it in the catalogue of that year as 'a charming and entertaining game for children', 'Busy Bees' has a honeycomb-shaped gameboard. The counters are Bees, and they work from cell to cell until they have called on all 4 flowers and collected a coloured Hive from each.

1 This is a game for 2–4 players, each of whom takes a Bee counter of a different colour. The 16 Hives are then distributed round the various flower panels according to colour, 4 to a panel. The object of the game is for the Bees to visit each of the flowers and collect 4 hives of different colours.

2 The order of play is determined by throwing the dice. The highest scorer begins, the second highest goes next, and so on.

3 The first player places his or her Bee on the centre spot and throws the dice. The Bee is then moved 2 cells through

numbered openings corresponding to the 2 numbers turned up by the dice. The

player may choose in which order to use the numbers, thereby in some measure controlling the Bee's flight.

4 Once the first Bee has moved off, the second Bee alights on the centre spot, the second player throws the dice and moves according to his or her preference. The other Bees follow, and play continues in rotation.

5 To visit a flower, and so claim a Hive, the Bee must enter 1 of the cells adjacent to a flower panel. The 2 cells at the corners on the centreline of the gameboard count as adjacent to either the flower above or the flower below, according to the

player's preference. After a Bee has visited a flower, it collects a Hive of that colour and resumes its quest from the centre spot. If a Bee can reach a flower with 1 of its moves, it may do so, and immediately begin again from the centre spot with the second move.

6 A Bee may not enter a cell occupied by another Bee. If a Bee is unable to move in either of its 2 possible directions, it must remain where it is and await its next chance.

7 The winner is the player whose Bee first collects 1 Hive from each of the flowers. Bees may not collect more than 1 Hive per flower.

MOUNT EVEREST

This 1923 game reflects the strong interest that the British, from their colonial base in India, have taken in the Himalayas – and especially in Mount Everest, at 29,028 feet (8,848 metres) the highest mountain in the world.

Straddling the Nepal–Tibet border, it was named after Sir George Everest (1790–1866), surveyor-general for India. Several climbing expeditions narrowly failed to reach the summit, including the fatal attempt by Mallory and Irvine in 1924, before it was eventually conquered in 1953 by a British-led party. First men to the top were Sir Edmund Hillary, a New Zealander, and Tenzing Norgay, a Sherpa guide and veteran mountaineer. The game is a race between Teams of 2 Mountaineers, who move 1 at a time, according to the players' preference, from the base camp to the Summit at No. 117. On their way they encounter various hazards. To win, both Mountaineers must safely reach the top.

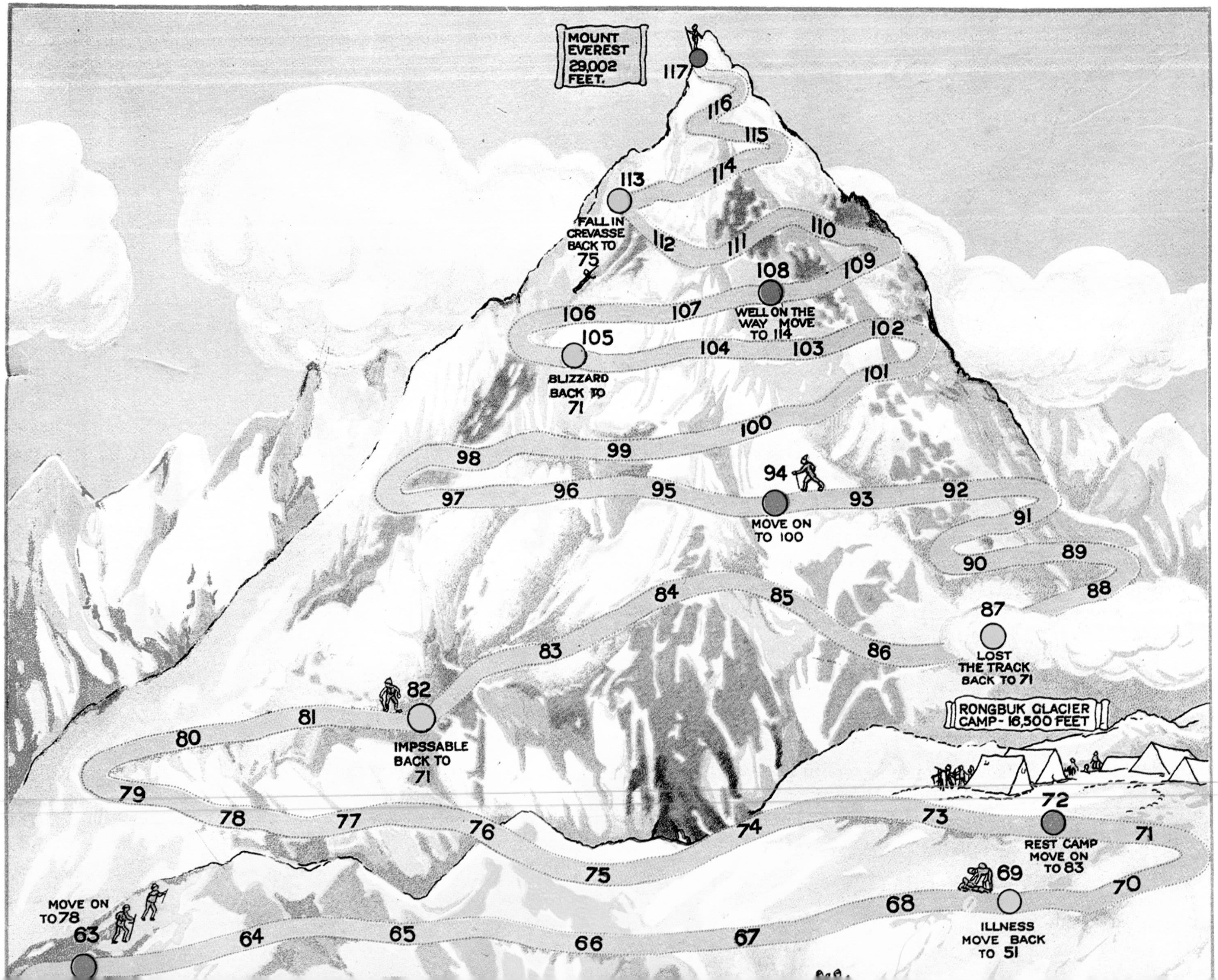

MOUNT EVEREST 29,002 FEET.

117
116
115
114
113 FALL IN CREVASSE BACK TO 75
112
111
110
109
108
107
106
105 BLIZZARD BACK TO 71
104
103
102
101
100
99
98
97
96
95
94 MOVE ON TO 100
93
92
91
90
89
88
87 LOST THE TRACK BACK TO 71
86
85
84
83
82 IMPASSABLE BACK TO 71
81
80
79
78
77
76
75
74
73
72
71
70
69 ILLNESS MOVE BACK TO 51
68
67
66
65
64
63 MOVE ON TO 78

WELL ON THE WAY MOVE TO 114

RONGBUK GLACIER CAMP – 16,500 FEET

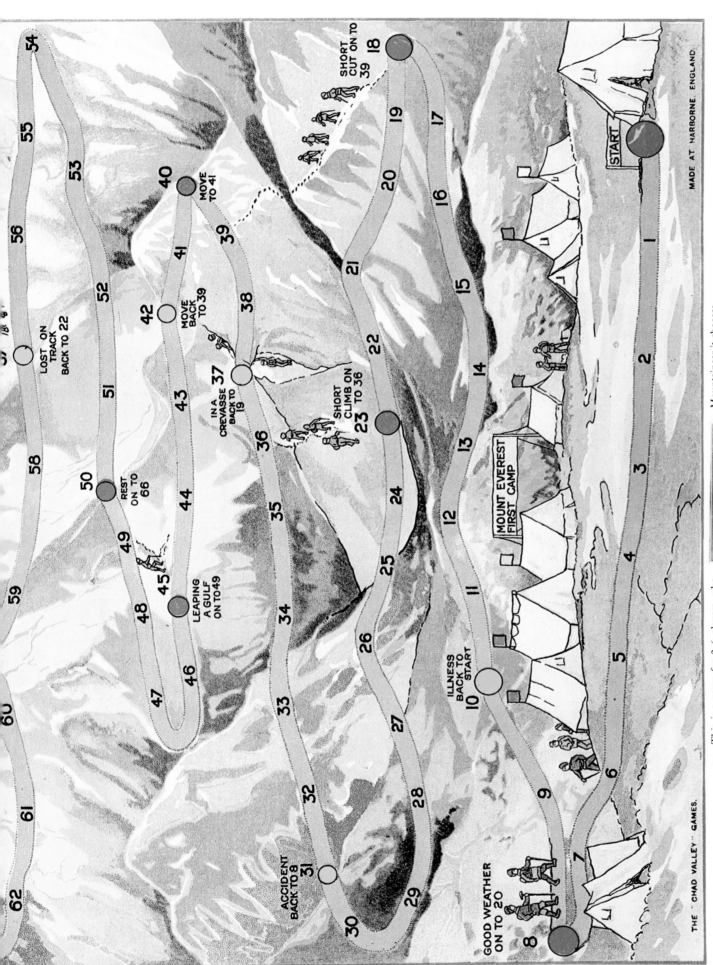

MADE AT HARBORNE, ENGLAND.

THE "CHAD VALLEY" GAMES.

54 55 53 56 52 51 58 50 49 59 48 45 60 47 46 61 62

LOST ON TRACK BACK TO 22

40 MOVE TO 41

42 MOVE BACK TO 39

41

39

38

REST ON TO 66

44

43

45 LEAPING A GULF ON TO 49

IN A CREVASSE 37 BACK TO 19

36

35

34

33

32

31 ACCIDENT BACK TO 8

30

29

28

27

26

25

24

SHORT CLIMB ON 23 TO 36

22

21

20

19

SHORT CUT ON TO 18 39

17

16

15

14

13

12

11

10 ILLNESS BACK TO START

9

8 GOOD WEATHER ON TO 20

7

6

5

4

3

2

1

START

MOUNT EVEREST FIRST CAMP

Mount Everest

1   This is a game for 2–6 players, who should divide themselves into Teams of 2 Mountaineers each, represented by the counters in 3 differently coloured sets. If there are only 2 players, they may prefer to operate 1 Team each, leaving the third colour aside. Each Team places its counters beside the Start position.

2   The order of play is determined by throwing the die. The highest scorer begins, the second highest goes next, and so on.

3   The Teams break camp at the Start by throwing the die in turn and each advancing 1 Mountaineer by the number indicated. Each Team may move whichever Mountaineer it chooses.

4   On their route to the Summit, Mountaineers arriving on a number marked by a circle must observe the instructions printed beside each of these. Mountaineers may overtake one another, but because of the hazardous nature of the route may not arrive on a number occupied by another Mountaineer, whether of the same Team or a Rival Team. Players so doing must return to their previous mark.

5   The winner is the Team that first gets its 2 Mountaineers to the Summit (No. 117). Here in each case the exact number required must be cast, i.e. the Summit may not be overshot.

77

SCOUTING

The gameboard of Chad Valley's 'Scouting' (1910) is designed to represent a tract of country crossed by paths running in all directions. A lone Despatch Runner sets off from the top of the board and tries to break through a cordon of Boy Scout opponents and deliver a message to a Field Officer at the foot of the board, armed with a reply to his notional message. Once more the Patrol of Scouts tries to stop him getting through. If he successfully avoids being hemmed in by the 'enemy' Patrol, the game is restarted by the Despatch Runner setting off for home from the foot of the board, armed with a reply to his notional message. Once more the Patrol of Scouts tries to stop him getting through. The game was produced at a time when the appeal of the Boy Scout movement, founded in 1908 by Lord Baden-Powell, was gathering momentum. Chad Valley brought out other games and kits aimed at helping Scouts and Scouting, among them 'Scout Tests' (1911), 'Scout Signaller' (1915), and 'Scout's Outfit' (1915).

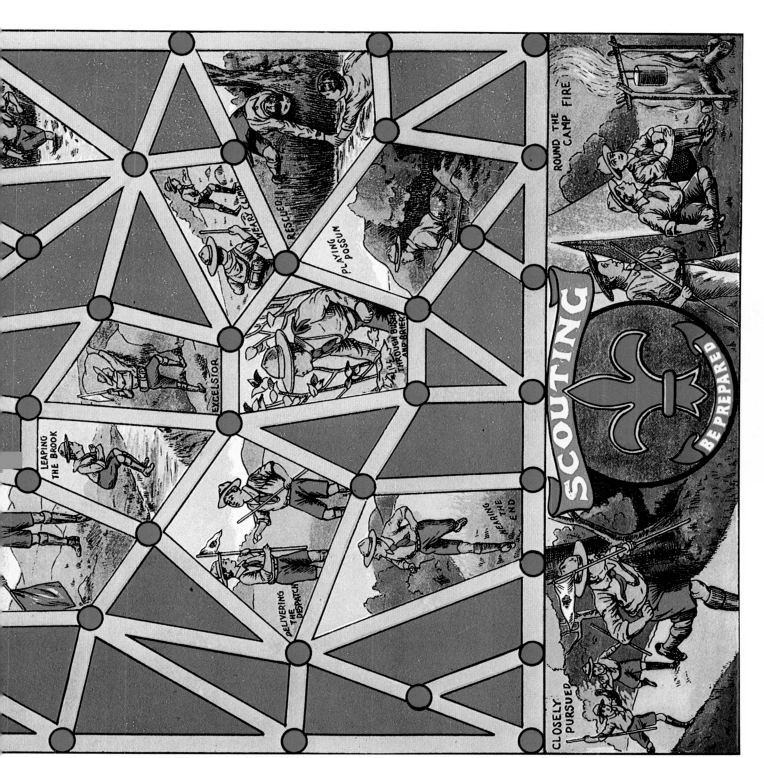

1 This is a game for 2, 3 or 4 players, or it may be played by a full Patrol of 8 Scouts. Should a full Patrol be playing, 1 member is chosen to be the Despatch Runner (Red), 6 play as individual Scouts (Blue), and the 8th man acts as Umpire to settle disputes. Each member of the Patrol takes his turn as Umpire.

2 The Red Despatch Runner is placed on the spot at the centre of the top of the board. The Blue Scouts occupy any 6 of the 8 spots at the bottom of the board.

3 The purpose of the game is for the Despatch Runner to deliver papers from a Field Officer at the top of the board to another at the bottom, and return with an answer. The Patrol of Scouts has been detailed to stop the Runner by hemming him in so that he cannot move – either on the outward journey or on the return home.

4 The Red Despatch Runner moves first, advancing by one spot. Each side then moves in turn. The Red Player may move backwards or forwards across the board, as he chooses; but the Blues may only move forwards or across, not back.

5 The 6 Blue players do not have to move their men in rotation. They may consult together to decide the most advantageous move.

6 If the Red player succeeds in reaching one of the bottom spots, he is then placed on the centre bottom spot in readiness for the return journey. The Blues are then removed to occupy any 6 spots at the top of the board. Play then proceeds as before, Red moving first.

7 The game is finished either when the Red Despatch Runner has completed the double journey, or when the Blue Scouts have captured him by so hemming him in in that he cannot move. A shorter version of the game may be played using the outward journey only.

QUARTETTE

A simple game to explain, but difficult to play – provided the opponents are evenly matched – 'Quartette' may be said to take the idea of 'Noughts and Crosses' a stage further by asking the players to place 4 pieces in line instead of 3. The game also has parallels with 'Draughts' and 'Chess' in that the pieces are set down in a formal arrangement before play begins, and are then moved 1 piece at a time, each player moving alternately, and trying to outwit his or her opponent.

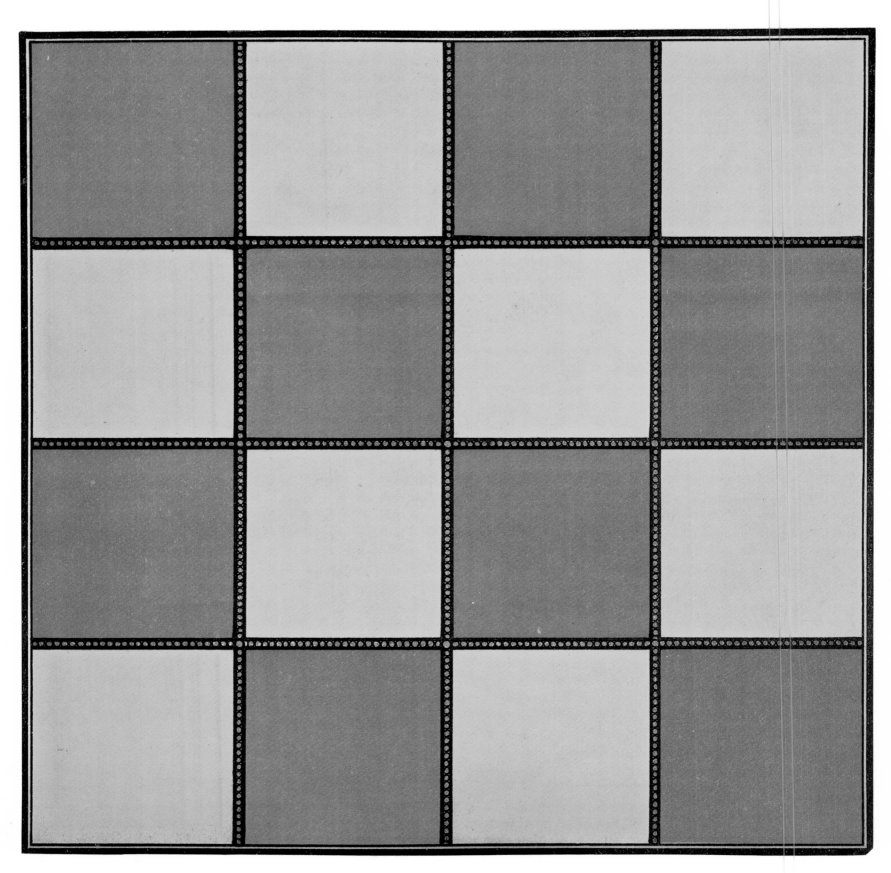

1 This is a game for 2 players, 1 of whom has 4 White pieces and the other 4 Black pieces. These 8 pieces are placed on the 2 opposite outer rows of squares on the board. They are laid down with White and Black alternating. A White piece always occupies the left-hand corner of each side.

2 The players move alternately, White beginning. At each turn, a player may move any one of his 4 pieces forwards, backwards or sideways – but not diagonally – into any unoccupied adjoining square.

3 Squares may not be skipped over, and a player must always make a move when it is his turn, whether to his advantage or not.

4 Each player aims to get his 4 pieces into a straight unbroken line – either laterally or diagonally in any direction.

5 The winner is the first player so to line up his 4 pieces.

HALMA

'Halma', or 'Alma' as it was originally called, dates from 1854, in which year the Battle of the Alma was fought in The Crimea. It has another, older derivation, being taken from the Greek word for 'jump'; as a 'jumping' game, 'Halma' is similar to 'Hoppity'.

This 1903 Chad Valley version of the game involves 2 players each with 10 counters which they try to transfer from their own Camp or Corner Enclosure to their opponent's before he or she can do the same. The original 'Halma' games offered a 2-handed version, in which each player had 19 counters, and a 4-handed version with 13 counters per player. The number of squares on the board remained consistent at 256, or 16 × 16.

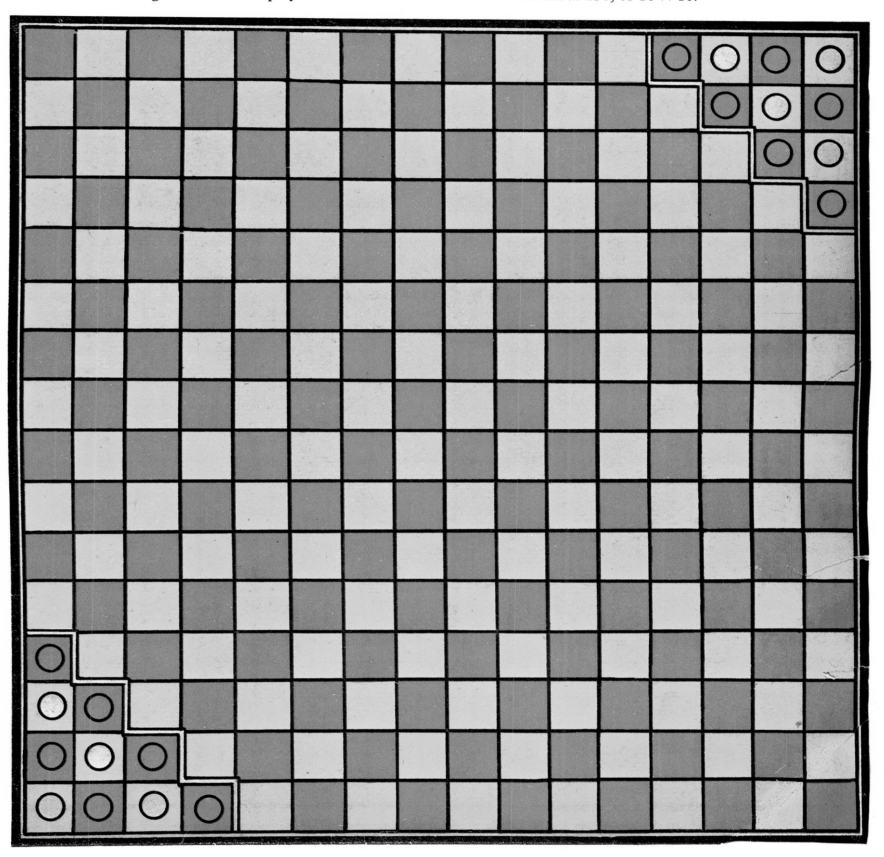

1 This is a game for 2 players. Each places his 10 counters in either of the 10-square Corner Enclosures. The object of the game is to move all 10 counters into the diagonally opposite corner.

2 Each player in turn moves 1 of his counters. The squares of both colours are used, and a counter may be moved either forwards, backwards or sideways into any adjoining vacant square.

3 Usually a counter may be moved only 1 square at a time. But if the adjoining square is occupied by another counter (whether his opponent's or his own), and there is a vacant square beyond, a player may jump his counter over the other and into the vacant square.

4 This hopping movement may be repeated any number of times, so long

as the chain of alternating counters and vacant squares continues, either in a straight or zig-zag path. It is up to the player, however, to decide how far along such a chain he shall move his counter.

5 Arising from the last rule, it will be found that a chain or ladder may be formed diagonally across the board, along which a counter may in 1 move be transferred from 1 Enclosure to the other. As a game develops, each player endeavours to use his opponent's ladder and to keep his opponent from using his.

6 Once a counter has passed into the opposite Corner Enclosure, it cannot be moved out again.

7 The winner is the player who first gets all his counters into the opposite corner.

FLIP-O-HOY

This aerial race game was published by Chad Valley in 1923. It consists of a 'sky track' divided into stages representing an actual flight.

Various hazards, both natural (Fog, for example) and mechanical (Spinning Nose Dive, Engine Trouble, etc.) may have to be dealt with on the way round. Scoring is determined by a spinning totum in the shape of a propeller, which is placed in the centre of the gameboard. The black tip indicates the score.

In the original game, the propeller was sunk in a pre-formed dip, which prevented it from tipping over on its side or spinning out of the circle. To re-create these conditions, players are advised to fix the pivot fairly loosely in some kind of stand, such as the upturned tray of a matchbox.

1 This is a game for 2-6 players, each of whom is equipped with a counter or Plane of a different colour which he places on the Taking Off line.

2 The order of play is determined by spinning the special Propeller in the centre of the gameboard. The player with the highest score goes first, the second highest goes next, and so on. When spinning for order of play, the word spaces (Climbing, Fog, etc.) are disregarded. If the arrow of the Propeller rests opposite one of these, the player spins again.

3 Players advance round the board by spinning the Propeller in turn and moving by the number of spaces indicated. If a player arrives on Climbing, he may move forward 3 spaces. If he arrives on Engine Trouble, he loses height and goes back 500 feet. If he hits Crash, he is out of the game. If he runs into the Air Pocket, he rises 400 feet to avoid it. If he encounters Loop the Loop, he must spin again; if the second spin produces a number, he may double it and move forward accordingly; if it produces a hazard (Engine Trouble, etc.) he must play accordingly. If he meets Fog, he misses a turn. If he arrives on Spinning Nose Dive, he must go back to 2,000 feet. If he makes a Forced Landing, he misses 2 turns and resumes. If he arrives on Glide Home, he may proceed direct to Landing.

4 The winner is the player who first passes the Landing mark. The exact score is not required, but players must not overshoot by more than 3; if they do, they must return to their previous mark and try again when next it is their turn to spin.

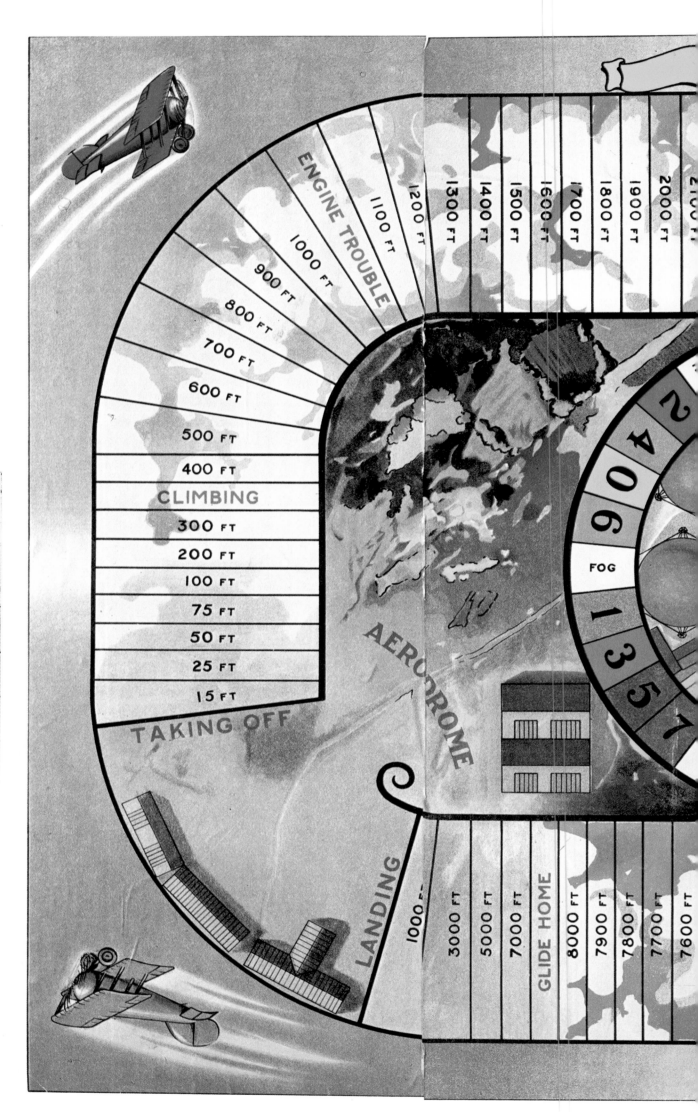

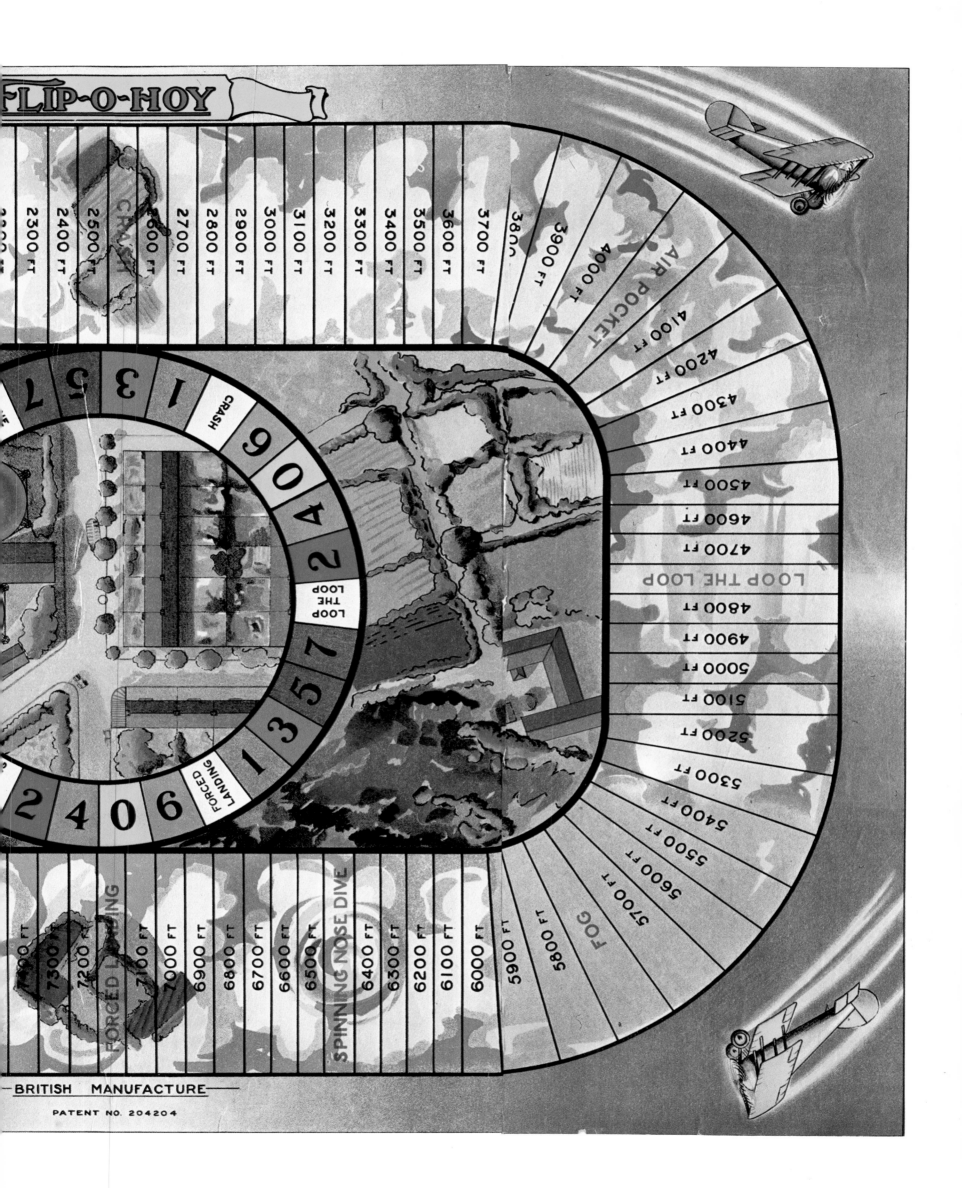

FLIP-O-HOY

CRASH

2300 FT
2400 FT
2500 FT
CRASH
2600 FT
2700 FT
2800 FT
2900 FT
3000 FT
3100 FT
3200 FT
3300 FT
3400 FT
3500 FT
3600 FT
3700 FT
3800 FT
3900 FT
4000 FT
AIR POCKET
4100 FT
4200 FT
4300 FT
4400 FT
4500 FT
4600 FT
4700 FT
LOOP THE LOOP
4800 FT
4900 FT
5000 FT
5100 FT
5200 FT
5300 FT
5400 FT
5500 FT
5600 FT
5700 FT
FOG
5800 FT
5900 FT
6000 FT
6100 FT
6200 FT
6300 FT
6400 FT
6500 FT
SPINNING NOSE DIVE
6600 FT
6700 FT
6800 FT
6900 FT
7000 FT
7100 FT
FORCED LANDING
7200 FT
7300 FT
7400 FT

CRASH
9 0 6
4
2
LOOP THE LOOP
1 3 5 7
1 3 5 7
FORCED LANDING
6 0 4 2
1 3 5 7

BRITISH MANUFACTURE

PATENT NO. 204204

GOLFO

'Golfo', basically a race game from 1–100, was published in 1910 by Chad Valley. In the adapted rules below, the first player to land on a hole, or pass it, picks up 1 token for that hole. The winner of the 18th Hole claims the remaining 3 tokens from the pool. The overall winner is the player with the most tokens. In the event of a tie, the leading scorers play off the last hole again.

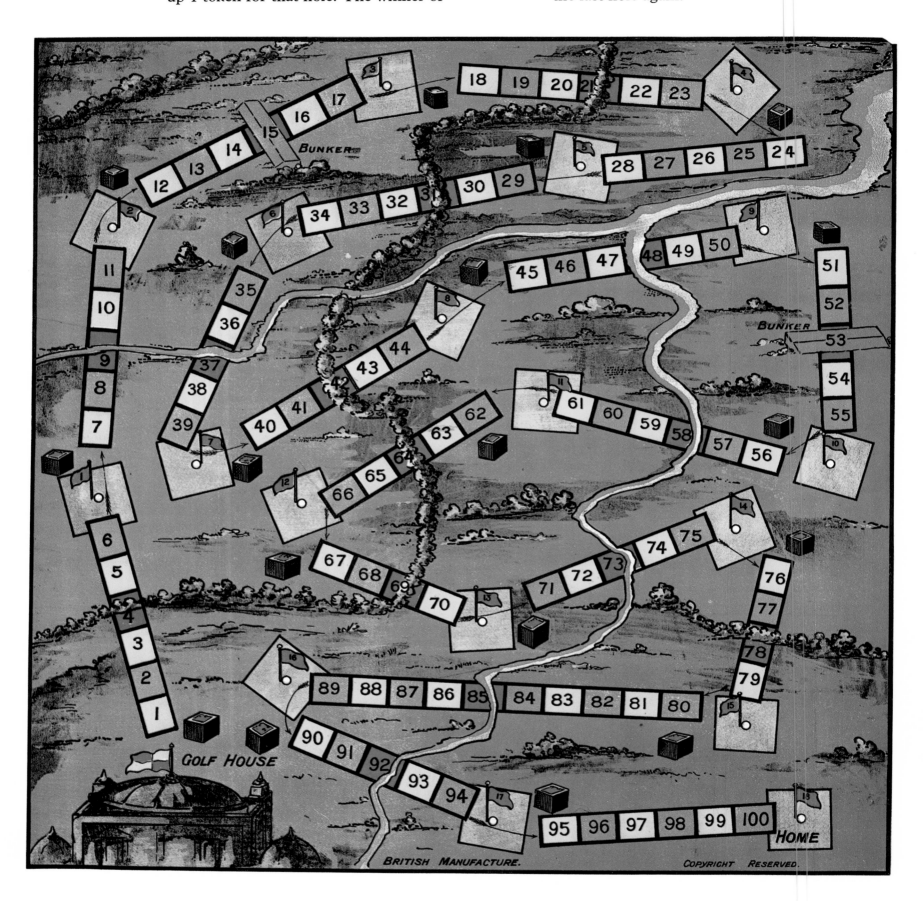

1 This is a game for 2–4 players, each of whom is provided with a counter of a different colour, which he places beside the Starting Tee near Golf House. Twenty tokens are placed in a pool, to be drawn by the winners of individual holes.

2 The order of play is determined by throwing the die. The highest scorer plays first, the second highest goes next, and so on.

3 The players throw the die in turn and advance by the number indicated. The first player to reach 6 wins Hole 1 and draws 1 token from the pool. This pattern of play is repeated round the course until all 18 holes have been played. The first player to reach 100 exactly wins Hole 18 and draws the remaining 3 tokens from the pool. If a player overshoots the 100 mark, he must

count up to 100 and then go backwards by the amount he has overshot. To win Holes 1–17, it is not necessary to score the exact number of the hole (6, 11, 17, etc.), and any excess may be counted against the next hole.

4 Around the Course are certain hazards. If a player lands in a hedge or bunker, he misses 1 turn. If he lands in a stream, he loses his ball and must miss a turn and tee off again from the start of that hole.

5 The winner is the player with the largest number of tokens, the count being made as soon as the first player has reached 100. In the event of a tie, the players concerned place their counters on the 18th Tee, beside No. 95, and play off the last hole again. The winner of the play-off is the first to score 100 exactly.

FOOTER

'The best indoor football game invented – highly popular with followers of the game.' Thus the Chad Valley catalogue for 1910.

Football, with its complex rules, is a difficult game to simulate, and Chad Valley and other manufacturers worked hard to outdo one another with games that were more 'real' or more exciting.

Mechanical action was increasingly favoured, and soon the most sought-after soccer games offered blowpipes, or miniature figures which could be moved round the field of play, and even be made to 'kick' the ball; such was the appeal of games like 'Goal Kick' and 'Blow Football' (both 1910), and 'Penalty Goal' (1925).

1 This is a game for 2 players, each of whom is provided with a counter of a different colour which he places over the ball in the centre of the field. Players should also agree in advance how many goals need to be scored to win the match, e.g. whether they should play to the best of 5, the first to score 5, or whatever.

2 The players toss a coin to determine the order of play. The winner kicks into the goal at the top of the board, the loser into the bottom goal.

3 The players throw a die in turn and advance towards their opponent's goal by the number indicated. A goal is scored by shooting past the goalkeeper (No. 25). If the shot is not big enough to carry beyond

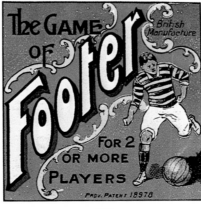

the goalkeeper and lands on 25, he saves it and punts the counter back upfield to 5.

4 Other hazards are as follows. If a player lands on 8 (Foul), he must return to Start. If he lands on 13 (Throw in), he may advance 2 spaces. If he lands on 22 (Penalty), he has a free shot at goal, and scores with a 3, 4, 5 or 6; if he throws a 1 or 2, the goalkeeper saves the shot and punts the counter back upfield to 5. If he lands on 24 (Offside), he must go back to 14.

5 When a goal is scored, both counters are replaced on the centre spot and the loser restarts play by throwing the die.

6 The winner is the player who first scores the match-winning number of goals agreed before the game.

BL'ND PIG

Two 'Farmers' battle to force their apparently 1-eyed, if not totally bl'nd, Pigs up the long road to Market. As in 'Marathon Race' (see pages 60–61), the route is a minefield of detours, and the only consolation that the Farmers may draw from having to control 2 Pigs rather than 1 is that they may choose, after throwing the dice, in which order the beasts shall be propelled nearer the finishing enclosure.

MARKET

50

THE 'CHAD VALLEY' GAMES

MADE AT HARBORNE, ENGLAND.

BL'ND P'G

LEFT · RIGHT

BL'ND P'G

WITHOUT ANY EYES

A GAME FOR 2 OR MORE PLAYERS

1 This is a game for 2 players, each of whom is provided with 2 Black or 2 White counters. One pair of counters, or Pigs, is played up the Left side of the board, the other up the Right side.

2 The order of play is determined by throwing the dice. The player with the higher number begins.

3 The players in turn throw the dice and advance 1 Pig by the score of 1 die, and the other Pig by the score of the other die. Players may choose how best to move their Pigs after they have thrown.

4 If the Pig arrives at the entrance to a field, marked IN, it must enter the field and be pushed all the way round until it reaches the OUT gate, where it resumes the direct route to Market. (The numbering in Fields 1–4 is somewhat arbitrary, but any Pig entering must go the whole way round.)

5 The winner is the player who first gets both Pigs to Market (No. 50). The exact number required must be cast, and the Pig is then placed in the Market pen, from which it may not wander. If a player scores more than the exact number required, he must advance his Pig up to 50 and then backwards by the amount of the excess. Once 1 Pig is in the Market pen, that player may only throw 1 die, not both, for his second Pig.

WHIRLPOOL

For the keen gamesplayer, 'Whirlpool'
offers the curiosity of a game that may be
won by throwing consistently <u>low</u> scores.
For others, it may be likened to a slow
bicycle race, with the added <u>frisson</u> of the
ever-present Vortex, which sucks all
players but 1 into its depths. He, or she,
having hung on the longest,
wins the game.

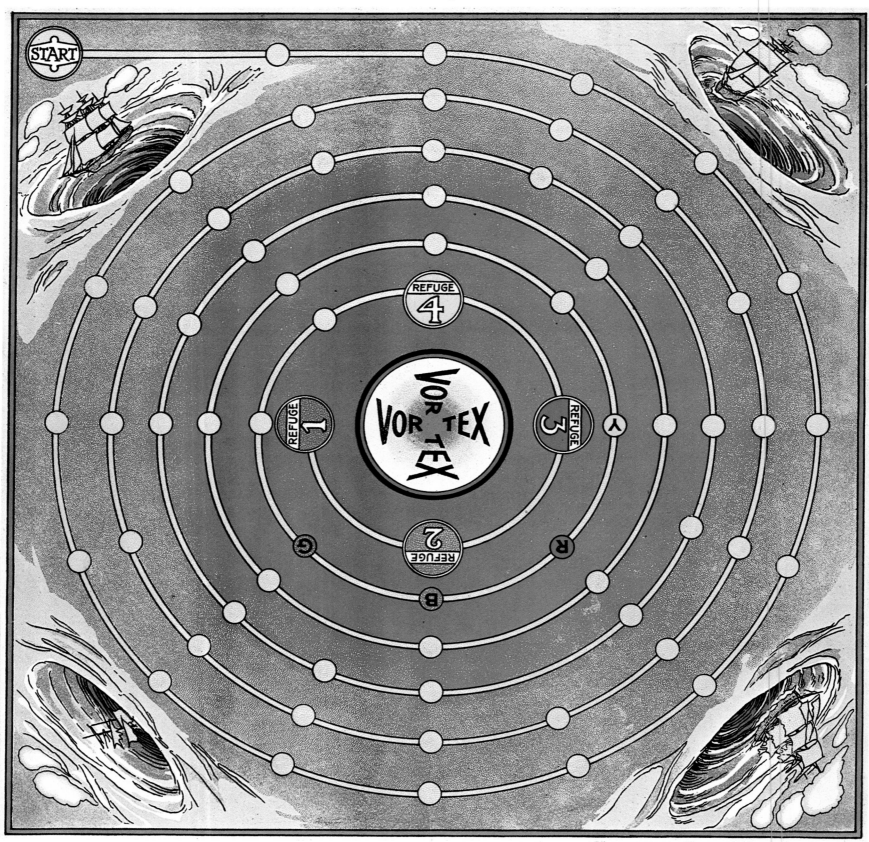

1 This is a game for 2–4 players, each of whom takes a counter of a different colour.

2 The order of play is determined by throwing the die. The highest scorer begins, the second highest goes next, and so on.

3 The players throw the die in turn and advance towards the Vortex by the amount indicated. Since the object of the game is to avoid being swept into the Vortex, low scores are the most desirable.

4 If a player lands on a space occupied by another player, they change places.

If, on nearing the centre of the board, a player lands on the marked circle of his

colour (Y, R, B, G), then he is carried immediately into the Vortex and is lost. If he lands on his correct Refuge (4 Yellow, 3 Red, etc.), he may shelter there until dislodged by throwing a 6. If he lands on the Refuge of another colour, he may shelter there and miss 1 turn provided he is not displaced by the proper owner; in which case, he is drawn into the Vortex. If, in the latter situation, a second player also of the wrong colour arrives on that Refuge, the 2 players change places.

5 The winner is the last player left outside the Vortex.

HARE & HOUNDS

'Hare & Hounds' (Chad Valley, 1922) is based upon a design patented in November 1890 by E.A.S. Fawcett. This was for a game called 'Dick Turpin's Ride to York'. Mr Fawcett's game in turn resembles 'Fox and Geese', 1 of a series of Norse games in which 2 groups of differing strength compete against each other. The present game is also similar to 'Scouting' (see pages 78–79), except that the course is 1-way, and the point of arrival more precisely defined.

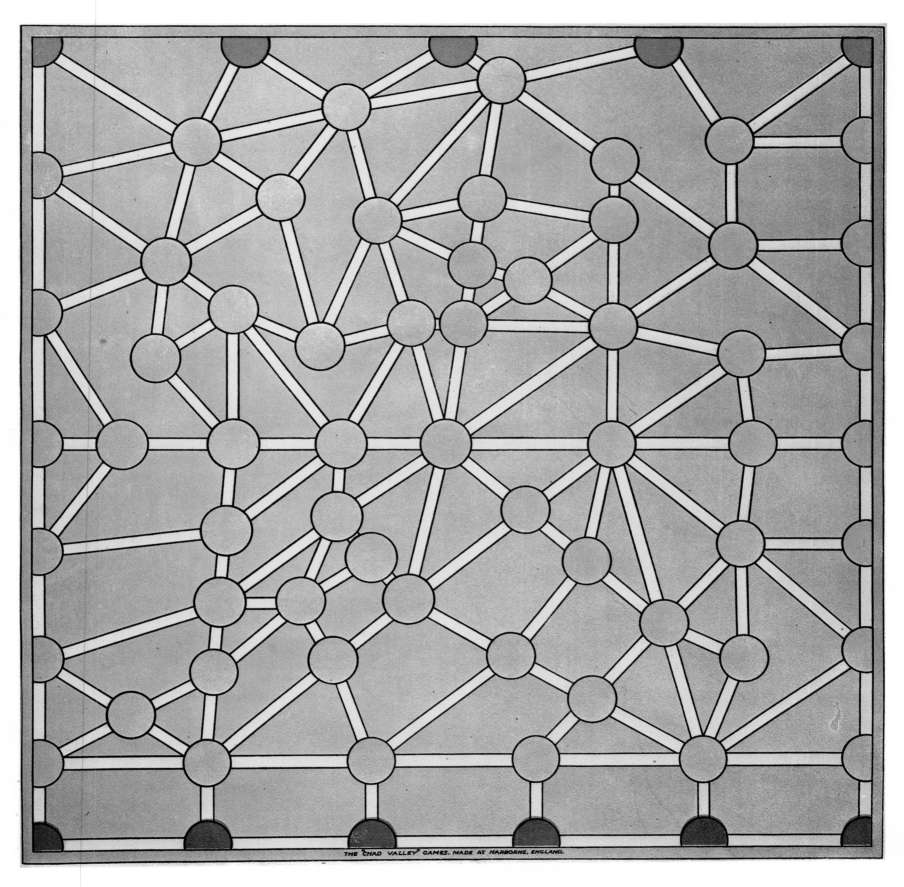

THE "CHAD VALLEY" GAMES. MADE AT HARBORNE. ENGLAND.

1   This is a game for 2–6 players. One is the Hare, and the other players control the 5 Hounds. The Red counter representing the Hare is placed on the centre spot at the top of the board, and the Blue Hounds occupy any 5 of the spots at the bottom of the board.

2   The object of the game is for the Hare to run past the Hounds and reach Home, which is either of the two centre spots at the bottom of the board.

3   The Hare begins, and may move 1 space at a time in any direction. The Hounds move 1 at a time, and may move in any direction except backwards. The Hounds need not move in rotation but in any order by common agreement.

4   The Hounds cannot 'take' the Hare but can defeat him by hemming him in so that he cannot move.

5   The game is finished either when the Hare reaches Home, or when the Hounds have trapped him so that he cannot move.

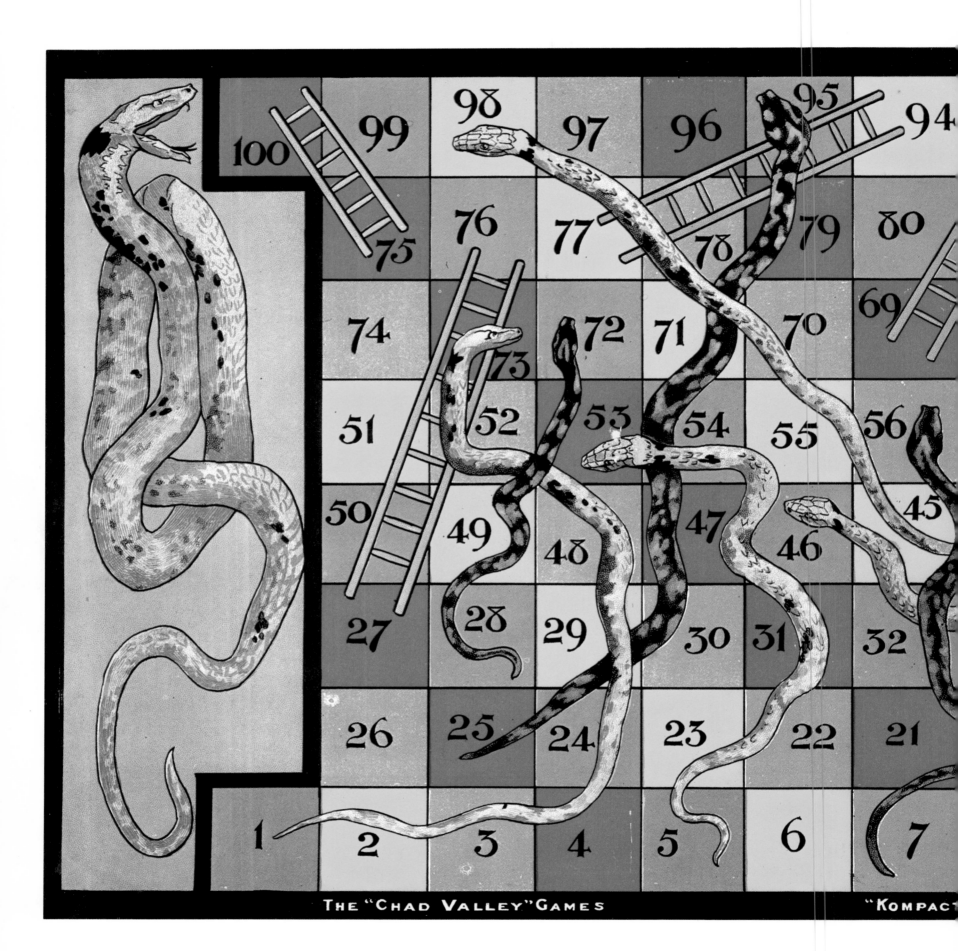

THE "CHAD VALLEY" GAMES

"KOMPACT

SNAKES & LADDERS 2

The transformation of 'Snakes & Ladders' from a circular (see pages 22–23) to a rectangular game began on 15 March 1893, when R.H. Harte, a journalist, patented his new design. The board he had devised was marked off into squares numbered 1–34; and fixed in the centre of the board

was a revolving totum numbered 1–10. In place of the traditional snakes, Harte introduced arrows (6 in all) for descending moves, but he retained ladders for moving upwards. Unlike most modern versions of the game, Harte's finished in the top right, rather than the top left, corner.

Many 'Snakes & Ladders' games were manufactured by Chad Valley from the turn of the century. The snake was restored, and a rectangular shape favoured. The board illustrated was published in 1911 under the Kompactum trademark; the artist evidently did not share Mr Harte's dislike of snakes.

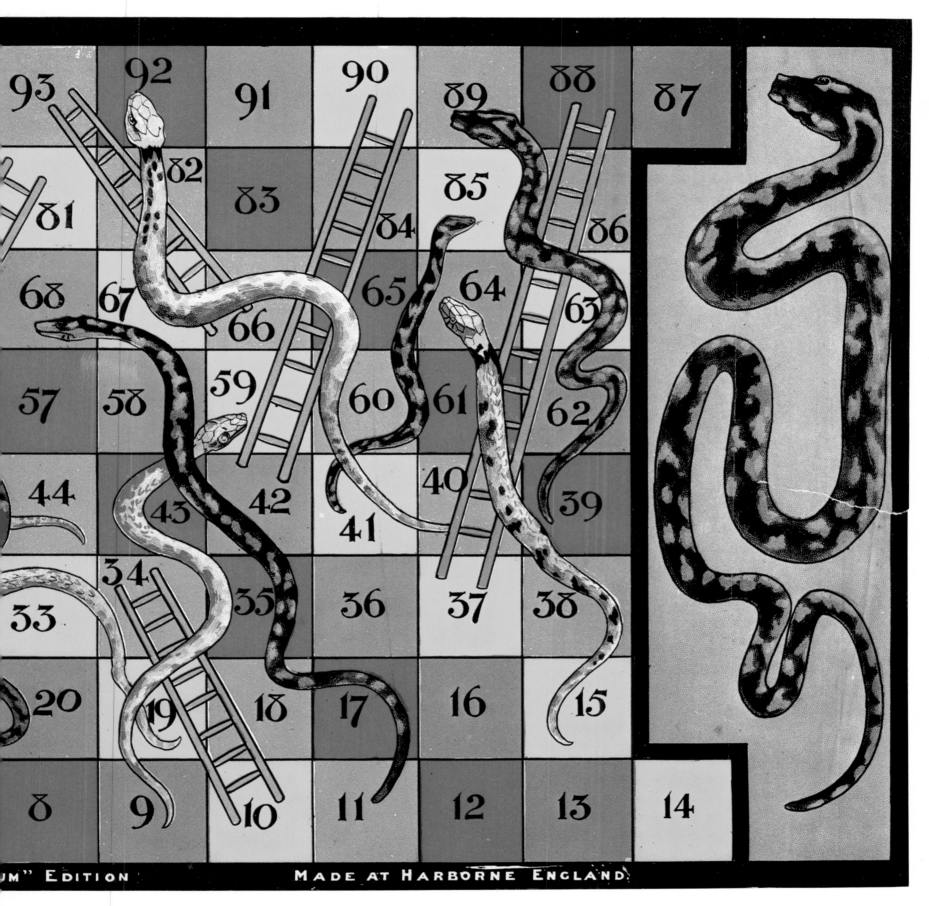

UM" EDITION   MADE AT HARBORNE ENGLAND

1 This is a game for 2–6 players. Each is provided with a counter of a different colour.

2 The order of play is determined by throwing the die. The highest scorer begins, the second highest goes next, etc.

3 The players throw the die in turn and advance by the number indicated. Players throwing a 6 are entitled to another turn (but not to a third throw if a second 6 is scored). Gradually the counters travel back and forth across the board, aiming for Square No. 100.

4 If a counter is played into a square from which a Ladder rises, it is carried

up and placed in the square at the top of the Ladder. If it is played into a square occupied by the head of a Snake, it is carried down to the square at the end of the Snake's tail. Counters are played freely across squares bearing other parts of the Ladders and the Snakes; these are regarded as conventional squares.

5 If a counter is played into a square occupied by another player's counter, it must be returned to its previous square.

6 The winner is the player who first gets to Square No. 100. The exact number required must be cast, i.e. the 100 mark must not be overshot.

AERIAL ATTACK

Produced in 1942, 'Aerial Attack' is in essence a race game from 1–60. It was a game for that special time, the blacked-out hours of the Blitz in Britain, when patriotism and survival were the closest of neighbours.

The rules, rewards and punishments are issued in the clipped tones that recall old newsreel commentaries, while the final share-out of the pool – ⅔ to the winner, ⅓ to the second player home – is certainly the only example of prize-rationing to appear in this book.

1 This is a game for 2–6 players, each of whom is provided with a counter of a different colour and an agreed number of tokens. All players should begin with the same number of tokens, and 12 are paid initially into the pool.

2 Players throw the die to determine the order of play. The highest scorer throws first, the second highest goes next, and so on.

3 Players must throw a 1 to start. They then advance by the number indicated, moving towards No. 60 in the course of the Air Raid. More than 1 player may occupy the same space, but all must observe the rulings that apply to particular spaces:
No. 2. Enemy aircraft (Black) approaching. Throw again.
No. 4. Alarm sounded in good time. Take 3 tokens for watchfulness.
No. 5. Our defence squadron (Red) rises to meet the enemy. Throw again.
No. 8. Dogfight in the sky. Stop to watch and miss a turn.
No. 14. Red plane shoots down enemy. Advance to 20.
No. 19. Black plane drops to earth, crew save themselves by parachute. Receive 2 tokens from the next player to throw.
No. 24. Severe thunderstorm compels Red flier to make emergency landing. Go back to 18.
No. 26. Black plane, trapped by balloon curtain, hurtles towards the ground. Go back to 1.
No. 30. Black and Red fliers collide. Miss 2 turns.
No. 34. Enemy plane turns to escape. Go back to 28.
No. 40. Incendiary bomb strikes basement room, cleared according to regulations. Receive 1 token from all other players.
No. 41. Fire extinguished according to regulations. Throw again.
No. 44. How not to fight a fire. Pay 5 tokens to pool.
No. 48. Citizens must not linger in streets during an Air Raid. Miss 2 turns.
No. 50. Aircraft shot down and burning. Player eliminated from game.
No. 53. Weathering an attack in gas-protected premises. Throw again.
No. 55. Reading by light of open flame during Air Raid. Miss 2 turns for carelessness.
No. 57. Ambulance Corps in protective clothing go about their work. Receive 2 tokens for heroism from all other players.
No. 60. Our defence squadron lands after successfully warding off danger.

4 The winner is the first player to reach No. 60; overshooting is allowed. The winner is entitled to two-thirds of the pool, the second player receives the rest.

BANKER

'Bookmaker' might be a fairer title for this gambling game, in which players bet on numbers and the bank pays out fixed odds according to the fall of 3 dice, or a totum spun 3 times. The game nevertheless exerts the compulsive pull of all such games of chance, and players may happily enjoy themselves for hours provided the bank changes hands at regular intervals, so giving each punter an opportunity to balance his or her books.

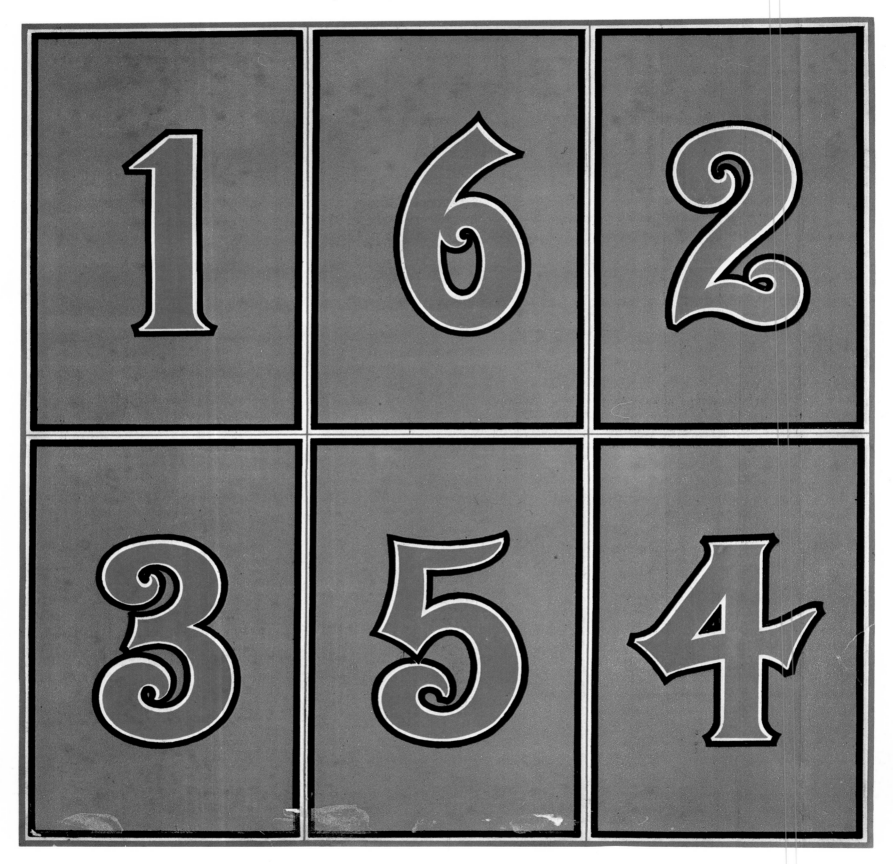

1 This is a game for 2 or more players, 1 of whom acts as Banker. Since the Banker usually wins, it is advisable to rotate this office after an agreed number of turns.

2 The players are provided with an equal number of tokens each, which they use to place bets on the number or numbers of their choice. To avoid disputes, it is as well if the Banker writes down the bets on a sheet of paper.

3 When all bets are placed, the Banker throws 3 dice, or spins a spinner 3 times. He then pays out as follows:
Evens on singles
2–1 on pairs
3–1 on 3 of a kind.